Determining Outcomes and Impacts of Human Resource Development Programs

Narong Kiettikunwong · Pennee Narot

Determining Outcomes and Impacts of Human Resource Development Programs

Springer

Narong Kiettikunwong
College of Local Administration
Khon Kaen University
Khon Kaen, Thailand

Pennee Narot
Faculty of Education
Khon Kaen University
Khon Kaen, Thailand

ISBN 978-981-97-0394-4 ISBN 978-981-97-0395-1 (eBook)
https://doi.org/10.1007/978-981-97-0395-1

This Springer imprint is published by the registered company Springer Nature Singapore Pte Ltd.
The registered company address is: 152 Beach Road, #21-01/04 Gateway East, Singapore 189721, Singapore

Preface

We extend a warm welcome to readers as they embark on an enlightening journey through the pages of this esteemed book, titled "Determining Outcomes and Impacts of Human Resource Development Programs." With utmost pleasure, we present this invaluable resource, designed to dive deeply into the conceptual framework, methodology, and practical application of an integrated evaluation model within the domain of human resource research.

In the contemporary world characterized by rapid transformations and interconnectedness, comprehending the outcomes and impacts of research projects holds paramount significance for informed decision-making, resource allocation, and societal advancement. Human resource development, with its multifaceted dimensions, profoundly shapes the trajectory of societies, economies, and individual lives. Consequently, evaluating the outcomes and impacts of human resource research assumes not only a necessity but also a responsibility to ensure the efficacy, efficiency, and sustainability of such endeavors.

This book draws upon a wealth of expertise and scholarly contributions to bridge the gap between theoretical frameworks and practical implementation, presenting a systematic and comprehensive approach to evaluate the outcomes and impacts of human resource research. At the core of this approach lies the recognition of three fundamental components that underpin human development: a long and healthy life, education and knowledge, and a decent standard of living. These components serve as guiding principles and a foundation for the integrated evaluation model, facilitating a holistic assessment of the multidimensional impacts of human resource research.

Embedded within the chapters of this book, readers will discover an exploration of diverse influencing contextual factors and their interplay with the integrated evaluation model. These factors encompass the content coverage and coherence of projects, the measurement of project worth, the evaluation of project impact, and the evaluation of project sustainability. Through meticulous discussions, insightful analyses, and thought-provoking examples, this book elucidates the practical application of the integrated evaluation model in real-world contexts, shedding light on its effectiveness and potential to instigate positive change.

As readers embark on this intellectually stimulating journey, we invite researchers, policymakers, practitioners, and stakeholders alike to immerse themselves in the wealth of knowledge presented within these pages. Each chapter serves as a roadmap for conducting comprehensive evaluations, guiding readers toward making informed decisions, enhancing project outcomes, and maximizing the positive impacts on individuals and society.

We extend our heartfelt gratitude to the esteemed contributors who have dedicated their expertise, insights, and experiences to this collaborative endeavor. Their collective wisdom and unwavering commitment have shaped this book into an invaluable resource poised to advance evaluation practices in the field of human resource development.

It is our fervent hope that readers find this book to be an enlightening and transformative companion, inspiring fresh perspectives, nurturing critical thinking, and fostering a culture of continuous improvement in the evaluation of human resource research.

We invite you to embark on this intellectual voyage, embracing the abundance of knowledge that lies ahead, as it illuminates your understanding of the outcomes and impacts of human resource research.

May this endeavor be both gratifying and enlightening.

Khon Kaen, Thailand

Narong Kiettikunwong
Pennee Narot

Contents

About the Authors

Narong Kiettikunwong is a faculty member in the College of Local Administration at Khon Kaen University, where he has been since 2014. He completed his undergraduate studies at Eastern Connecticut State University, earning a Bachelor of Science degree in Business Administration. Subsequently, he pursued a Bachelor of Laws (LL.B.) degree at Chulalongkorn University, followed by postgraduate studies in Master of Public Administration at the same institution. He further expanded his academic endeavors by obtaining a Master of Laws (LL.M.) in Competition & Regulation from Leuphana Universität Lüneburg. Notably, Narong is also an attorney-at-law. Before joining the college, Narong gained valuable experience working with the US Department of State and holding various positions in private companies, including his own venture, where he served as a founder and CEO. Currently, he contributes as an editor and author of collective monographs, demonstrating his active involvement in academic publications. His most recent scientific peer-reviewed book explores the topics of Education for the Elderly in the Asia Pacific and Interdisciplinary Perspectives on Special and Inclusive Education in a Volatile, Uncertain, Complex & Ambiguous (Vuca) World. Narong's research interests primarily revolve around public administration, digital government, and performance measurement. These areas of focus highlight his dedication to studying and advancing knowledge in the realm of governance and technology.

Pennee Narot retired after 30 years as Associate Professor in International and Development Education at the Faculty of Education, Khon Kaen University, Thailand. She holds a Ph.D. in International and Development Education from the University of Pittsburgh. Throughout her academic career, she has focused on teaching and conducting research in various areas, including teachers' development, non-formal and informal education, inclusive education, and analysis of aged situations in society. Pennee has dedicated her research efforts to the field of inclusive education, with a particular emphasis on enhancing the competency of students with special needs. Her work includes the development of professional learning programs aimed at improving the skills and capabilities of students with special needs. She has also conducted extensive research on inclusive education practices in Thailand, exploring different approaches and paths toward inclusion. Additionally, Pennee has investigated the role of special teachers as leaders in the development and promotion of inclusive education. Throughout her career, Pennee has been actively involved in research, contributing valuable insights to the field of inclusive education. Her work has significantly contributed to the understanding and advancement of inclusive education practices in Thailand.

List of Figures

List of Tables

Chapter 1
Introduction

In today's fast-paced and dynamic business environment, organizations face intense competition, rapidly evolving markets, and disruptive technological advancements. These factors have profoundly impacted the way organizations operate, strategize, and strive for success (Appelbaum et al., 2017).

The first factor, intense competition, is considered a hallmark of the contemporary business landscape. Globalization has eliminated geographical barriers and opened up markets to organizations worldwide. The rise of e-commerce platforms such as Amazon, Alibaba, eBay, and many more has significantly intensified competition in the retail sector. These platforms enable sellers and buyers from different countries to engage in trade (López González & Jouanjean, 2017).

As a result, retailers face fierce competition not only from local competitors but also from international players (Ramazanov et al., 2021). This has forced traditional brick-and-mortar retailers to adapt and develop their online presence to remain competitive. The intense competition in the e-commerce industry has led to constant innovation, price competition, and enhanced customer experiences as organizations strive to differentiate themselves and capture a market share.

Likewise, in the automotive industry, globalization has created intense competition among manufacturers. With the ability to export and import vehicles across borders, automakers face competition from both domestic and international players. For example, Japanese automakers like Toyota, Honda, and Nissan have expanded their operations globally, competing with traditional American and European manufacturers. Additionally, emerging economies such as China and India have entered the global automotive market, introducing new players and increasing competition further. Automakers must continuously innovate and improve their product offerings, focusing on quality, safety, fuel efficiency, and advanced technologies to gain a competitive edge. Globalization has also enabled consumers to have access to a wider range of vehicle options, creating a highly competitive environment in which automakers strive to attract customers and expand their market share.

N. Kiettikunwong and P. Narot, *Determining Outcomes and Impacts of Human Resource Development Programs*, https://doi.org/10.1007/978-981-97-0395-1_1

Secondly, rapidly evolving markets are a defining characteristic of business environments. Organizations must navigate through these markets to stay competitive, seize opportunities, and sustain their growth in the face of intense competition and disruptive technological advancements. One key aspect of rapidly evolving markets is the speed at which market conditions and customers' preferences change. Consumers' tastes, needs, and expectations are constantly evolving, driven by factors such as changing demographics, emerging trends, and technological advancements (Prasetio, 2022). As a result, organizations must continuously monitor market trends, conduct market research, and gather customers' insights to stay abreast of these evolving preferences. By understanding the changing landscape, organizations can adapt their products, services, and strategies to meet customers' demands, maintain their relevance, and capture potential new markets.

Thirdly, embracing disruptive technological advancements comes with its own set of challenges. Organizations must navigate issues related to data security, privacy, and ethical considerations as technology becomes increasingly integrated into various aspects of business operations (Martin et al., 2022). Additionally, organizations must ensure that they have the necessary technological infrastructure, talent, and capabilities to effectively adopt and leverage these advancements. For instance, the rise of the sharing economy, enabled by platforms such as Uber and Airbnb, has disrupted traditional industries such as transportation and hospitality. These platforms leverage technology to connect individuals and enable peer-to-peer transactions, challenging established players and offering innovative alternatives. Organizations need to be aware of these emerging business models and technologies to identify new opportunities for growth, collaboration, and market expansion. Thus, organizations must adapt their strategies to meet the demands of digitally savvy consumers who expect seamless online experiences, personalized recommendations, and quick delivery options (Rigby, 2011).

By leveraging disruptive technologies, organizations can enhance their customer engagement, create immersive experiences, and gain a competitive advantage. To effectively address this challenge, organizations must focus on key strategies, such as identifying the essential skills and competencies needed for successful technological implementation, fostering the attraction and retention of talent with expertise in emerging technologies, and developing comprehensive training programs to enhance the skill sets of their existing workforces (Kristoffersen et al., 2021). These initiatives can serve as the cornerstone for achieving success in the face of disruptive technological advancements.

The points outlined above demonstrate how intense competition resulting from globalization has both positive and negative implications. On the positive side, it drives innovation, fosters continuous improvement, and promotes efficiency as organizations strive to outperform their rivals. Competition can also benefit consumers by offering a wider range of products, better quality, and competitive pricing. However, intense competition can also create challenges for organizations. It requires significant investments in research and development, marketing, and strategic initiatives to stay ahead of the competition and, most importantly, in human resource development (HRD) to keep up with constantly changing market dynamics, consumers' preferences, and emerging technologies so as to maintain a competitive edge. Failure to do so may result in lost market share, reduced profitability, and potential business failure.

The Current State of HRD

The current state of HRD is influenced by several factors, such as globalization, technological advancement, demographic shifts, economic fluctuations, social and environmental issues, and changing customer expectations. These factors pose both opportunities and challenges for HRD practitioners and researchers. On one hand, they create a need for continuous learning and innovation to cope with the dynamic and complex environment. On the other hand, they require a strategic and holistic approach to align HRD initiatives with the organizational vision and mission.

The status quo of HRD is characterized by several trends and issues that reflect the changing nature of work and the workforce, as well as the evolving needs and expectations of organizations and individuals. One of the most prominent trends in HRD is the increasing use of digital technologies and platforms for delivering and facilitating learning and development. These technologies include e-learning, mobile learning, gamification, social media, artificial intelligence, virtual reality, augmented reality, and more. They offer learners and trainers with flexibility, accessibility, interactivity, personalization, and feedback. For instance, e-learning enables learners to access online courses and resources anytime and anywhere, and to learn at their own pace and style. Mobile learning allows learners to use their smartphones or tablets to access bite-sized and just-in-time learning activities, such as quizzes, videos, or podcasts. Gamification applies game design principles and mechanics to learning activities to make them more engaging, motivating, and rewarding. Social media enables learners to connect and share with each other and with experts, and to co-create and co-evaluate learning resources. Artificial intelligence, virtual reality, and augmented reality provide learners with immersive and realistic learning experiences that simulate real-world situations and challenges. However, the increasing use of digital technologies and platforms for HRD also poses several challenges and risks that need to be addressed. These challenges include ensuring the quality and relevance of learning resources and activities, protecting the security and privacy of learners and trainers, ensuring the ethical use of data and algorithms, and evaluating the effectiveness and impact of learning outcomes.

Another trend in HRD is the growing demand for lifelong learning and career adaptability. As the world of work changes rapidly and unpredictably, employees and managers need to constantly update their skills and competencies to remain relevant and competitive. This requires a shift from a linear and fixed career path to a nonlinear and flexible one that allows for career exploration, transition, and development across the lifespan. HRD practitioners and researchers need to design and implement programs that support lifelong learning and career adaptability, such as competency-based education, personalized learning plans, micro-credentials, apprenticeships, mentorship, and coaching. Diversity and inclusion are also becoming increasingly important issues in HRD, as they are key drivers of organizational performance and social responsibility. Diversity refers to the differences among people in terms of their demographic characteristics (such as age, gender, race, ethnicity, religion, disability), as well as their cognitive styles, values, beliefs, preferences, and experiences. Inclusion refers to the extent to which people feel valued, respected, accepted, and empowered in their work environment. HRD practitioners and researchers need to foster a culture of diversity and inclusion that leverages the strengths and perspectives of all employees and stakeholders, and that recognizes and addresses the barriers and biases that hinder the full participation and contribution of diverse groups.

Finally, HRD professionals themselves are facing new roles and competencies that reflect the strategic and integrated nature of HRD within organizations. HRD professionals need to acquire new skills and knowledge to perform their roles effectively, such as strategic partnership, change management, consulting, coaching, facilitation, research, evaluation, and innovation. They also need to develop new competencies that reflect the changing needs and expectations of organizations and individuals, such as business acumen, analytical thinking, communication, collaboration, creativity, critical thinking, emotional intelligence, ethical awareness, and cultural sensitivity. HRD professionals need to adapt to the changing landscape of HRD and to become lifelong learners themselves.

Critical Role of HRD

One of the key reasons why HRD is vital in the face of intense competition is its ability to facilitate organizational agility and adaptability (Mohrman, 2007). As market conditions change rapidly, organizations must be able to respond swiftly and effectively to shifting customers' preferences, emerging technologies, and competitive threats. HRD initiatives, such as training and development programs, enable employees to acquire new skills, enhance their expertise, and stay updated on industry trends. This empowers organizations to adapt their strategies, processes, and products/services in line with evolving market demands (Rosário & Raimundo, 2021).

Furthermore, HRD plays a critical role in fostering innovation and creativity within organizations (Hirudayaraj & Matić, 2021). In an intensely competitive environment, innovation is often the key differentiator that sets organizations apart from their rivals. HRD initiatives can cultivate a culture of innovation by promoting continuous learning, encouraging the generation of new ideas, and providing employees with the necessary tools and resources to experiment and think creatively. Through HRD, organizations can tap into the diverse talents and perspectives of their workforces, driving innovation and enabling them to introduce novel products, services, and business approaches that meet the customers' needs and surpass their competitors' offerings (Djikhy & Moustaghfir, 2019).

HRD contributes to the development of skilled and competent workforces, which are essential for maintaining high-quality products or services. Intense competition demands that organizations continually improve their operational processes, enhance product/service quality, and deliver exceptional customer experiences. HRD initiatives, such as skills' training, performance management, and career development programs, equip employees with the necessary competencies to excel in their roles, meet customer expectations, and contribute to organizational success. By investing in HRD, organizations can ensure that their workforces remain adaptable, competent, and capable of delivering superior value to customers (Ahmed et al., 2022).

Additionally, HRD facilitates effective talent management and employee retention in the face of intense competition. In a competitive marketplace, attracting and retaining top talent is critical for organizations seeking to outperform their rivals. HRD practices, including talent acquisition strategies, succession planning, leadership development, and employee engagement initiatives, contribute to creating a desirable work environment and fostering employees' loyalty. By investing in the development and well-being of their employees, organizations can enhance their employees' satisfaction, increase retention rates, and secure a competitive advantage through a talented and committed workforce (Islam & Amin, 2021).

It can be said that intense competition necessitates a strategic focus on HRD as a crucial element for organizational success because HRD enables organizations to navigate rapidly evolving market dynamics, embrace innovation, develop skilled workforces, and attract top talent. Investing in HRD initiatives such as training, development, talent management, and employee engagement, means that organizations can enhance their competitiveness, improve product/service quality, and deliver exceptional customer experiences. In this way, HRD becomes a key driver in helping organizations maintain a competitive edge and thrive in the face of intense market competition.

Despite its significance, there is a noticeable lack of research that specifically focuses on measuring the outcomes and impacts of HRD initiatives. Moreover, there is still a lack of clarity regarding the precise definition of outcomes and impacts arising from HRD, which has resulted in academic disagreements and varying conclusions. Establishing a suitable and agreed-upon definition is crucial to enable the evaluation of the impact potential of different HRD research initiatives. This distinction helps determine which research efforts are likely to contribute significantly to the expected impact and which may not yield substantial outcomes. Another point is that the provision of a framework for measuring the effectiveness of organizations' human resource efforts by evaluating the outcomes and impacts of human resource initiatives and addressing any gaps is a rare concept. By evaluating these outcomes and impacts, organizations can gain valuable insights into the effectiveness of their strategies, identify areas for improvement, and make data-driven decisions to enhance their human resource practices.

About This Book

This book consists of ten chapters each of which addresses different aspects of the evaluation topic, as follows.

Chapter 1 Introduction

This chapter provides an introduction to the importance of human resource research in enabling organizations to develop and sustain a competitive edge in the market. It also highlights the significance of evaluating the outcomes and impacts of human resource research.

Chapter 2 Overview of Human Resource Research

This chapter presents a comprehensive overview of human resource research, including its various types and the significance it holds for organizations. It delves into the challenges faced by organizations when it comes to measuring the outcomes and impacts of such research.

Chapter 3 Overview of Evaluations

This chapter serves as a valuable resource for evaluators, providing a comprehensive overview of evaluation research. It outlines the key steps involved in conceptualizing, implementing, and assessing programs, offering practical guidance to evaluators on how to effectively evaluate programs and make informed decisions. By following these steps, evaluators can enhance the quality and impact of their evaluation research, ultimately contributing to the improvement and success of programs and initiatives.

Chapter 4 Concept of Program Evaluation

This chapter discusses the diverse range of program evaluation approaches and highlights the appropriate tools to be employed in each approach. It also provides insights into the evaluation model's process, offering a comprehensive understanding of how evaluations are conducted.

Chapter 5 Implications of the Theory of Change in Program Evaluation

This chapter explores the integration of the Theory of Change (ToC) and Logic Model, highlighting their versatility, strengths, and limitations. It highlights the importance of alignment and adaptability within the ToC framework, offering a practical case study. The chapter covers program planning aspects like goals, inputs, intermediate outcomes, and short-term outcomes. It provides practical insights into using ToC and Logic Model for effective program development and evaluation.

Chapter 6 A Critical Examination of Kirkpatrick, Bushnell, Warr et al., and Stufflebeam and Zhang's Evaluation Models

This chapter explores the evaluation of human resource training programs by exploring, critiquing, and comparing four notable evaluation models: Kirkpatrick, Bushnell, Warr et al., and Stufflebeam and Zhang, among others. The objective is to offer a comprehensive understanding of the strengths and limitations of each model, helping HR practitioners and organizational leaders enhance their program evaluation methodologies. By aligning HR training programs with organizational goals and strategies, the chapter contributes to the improvement of HR practices and overall organizational performance.

Chapter 7 Determining Outcomes and Impacts of Human Resource Research with Participatory Evaluation

This chapter explores Participatory Evaluation's role in enhancing organizational effectiveness in today's complex and unpredictable business landscape. It discusses the benefits, including stakeholder engagement and flexibility in adapting evaluation methods, while acknowledging challenges. The chapter addresses the importance of aligning the evaluation model with specific issues to maximize its impact, fostering adaptability and innovation in a changing world.

Chapter 8 The Need for an Integrated Evaluation Model

This chapter elucidates the significance of employing an integrated evaluation model to effectively measure the outcomes and impacts of human resource research. It explores the advantages of adopting an integrated approach, encompassing the assessment of both short-term and long-term outcomes and impacts. Furthermore, the chapter outlines the key components of the integrated evaluation model designed for measuring the outcomes and impacts of human resource research.

Chapter 9 Methodological Framework for Evaluating Human Resource Research

This chapter provides detailed insights into the sequential steps involved in the evaluation process, including goal setting, objective establishment, method selection, and data analysis. It highlights the key elements and components of the framework and explains how they contribute to a rigorous and reliable evaluation process. Additionally, it emphasizes the importance of systematic and rigorous data collection to ensure the reliability and validity of the evaluation findings.

Chapter 10 Practical Illustration and Future Direction of the Integrated Evaluation Model

This chapter provides a concrete demonstration of the integrated evaluation model in action, showcasing its efficacy in assessing outcomes and impacts in human resource research. It emphasizes the model's effectiveness, valuable insights gained, and significance in evaluating interventions. The chapter also addresses limitations, offers recommendations for improvement, and highlights its contribution to the field's advancement.

In writing this book, the authors' aim is to provide a comprehensive handbook that serves as a valuable resource for various stakeholders, including organizational managers, consultants, investors, policymakers responsible for shaping the non-profit sector, and students and fellow researchers. The book not only offers an introduction to the integrated evaluation model for measuring the outcomes and impacts of human resource research but also highlights its potential applications. At the same time, it emphasizes the importance of recognizing the limitations and risks associated with practical implementation, cautioning against the dubious or unsystematic use of the methodology.

References

Ahmed, W., Hizam, S. M., & Sentosa, I. (2022). Digital dexterity: Employee as consumer approach towards organizational success. *Human Resource Development International, 25*(5), 631–641.

Appelbaum, S. H., Calla, R., Desautels, D., & Hasan, L. (2017). The challenges of organizational agility (part 1). *Industrial and Commercial Training, 49*(1), 6–14.

Djikhy, S., & Moustaghfir, K. (2019). International faculty, knowledge transfer, and innovation in higher education: A human resource development perspective. *Human Systems Management, 38*(4), 423–431.

Hirudayaraj, M., & Matić, J. (2021). Leveraging human resource development practice to enhance organizational creativity: A multilevel conceptual model. *Human Resource Development Review, 20*(2), 172–206.

Islam, M. S., & Amin, M. (2021). A systematic review of human capital and employee well-being: Putting human capital back on the track. *European Journal of Training and Development, 46*(5/6), 504–534.

Kristoffersen, E., Mikalef, P., Blomsma, F., & Li, J. (2021). Towards a business analytics capability for the circular economy. *Technological Forecasting and Social Change, 171*, 120957.

López González, J., & Jouanjean, M. (2017). *Digital trade: Developing a framework for analysis* (OECD Trade Policy Papers, No. 205). OECD Publishing, Paris, France. https://doi.org/10.1787/524c8c83-en

Martin, K., Shilton, K., & Smith, J. E. (2022). Business and the ethical implications of technology: Introduction to the symposium. In *Business and the ethical implications of technology* (pp. 1–11). Springer Nature.

Mohrman, S. A. (2007). Designing organizations for growth: The human resource contribution. *Human Resource Planning, 30*(4), 34.

Prasetio, E. A. (2022). Investigating the influence of network effects on the mechanism of disruptive innovation. *Journal of Open Innovation: Technology, Market, and Complexity, 8*(3), 157.

Ramazanov, I. A., Panasenko, S. V., Cheglov, V. P., Krasil'nikova, E. A., & Nikishin, A. F. (2021). Retail transformation under the influence of digitalisation and technology development in the context of globalisation. *Journal of Open Innovation: Technology, Market, and Complexity, 7*(1), 49.

Rigby, D. (2011). The future of shopping. *Harvard Business Review, 89*(12), 65–76.

Rosário, A., & Raimundo, R. (2021). Consumer marketing strategy and E-commerce in the last decade: A literature review. *Journal of Theoretical and Applied Electronic Commerce Research, 16*(7), 3003–3024.

Chapter 2
Overview of Human Resource Research

Introduction

Human resource research plays a crucial role in organizations by providing valuable insights into various aspects of the workforce (Kareem, 2019; Sinambela et al., 2022). It encompasses a broad spectrum of investigations that aim to understand and improve the dynamics of the workforce. Workforce dynamics refers to the intricate interplay of factors that influence employees' behavior, attitudes, performance, and overall engagement within an organization. These dynamics are shaped by a multitude of factors, including organizational culture, leadership styles, employee motivation, teamwork, diversity and inclusion, training and development, and the broader socio-economic environment. Human resource research provides valuable tools and methodologies to examine these factors, uncover underlying patterns, and make data-driven decisions to improve the dynamics within the workforce. Figure 2.1 illustrates the interplay among the workforce dynamics factors.

Organizational Culture

The culture of an organization greatly influences the behavior and attitudes of its employees (Naveed et al., 2022). One notable real-life example that highlights the significant influence of organizational culture on employee behavior and attitudes is the tech giant Google.

Google has cultivated a distinct and renowned culture that has become synonymous with its brand identity. The company places a strong emphasis on fostering a unique work environment that encourages creativity, collaboration, and individual autonomy. At Google, employees are provided with an array of perks and benefits, such as on-site gourmet meals, flexible work hours, and recreational spaces. The company's open office layout and informal dress code create a relaxed and

N. Kiettikunwong and P. Narot, *Determining Outcomes and Impacts of Human Resource Development Programs*, https://doi.org/10.1007/978-981-97-0395-1_2

Fig. 2.1 Workforce dynamics factors

comfortable atmosphere, where employees feel empowered to express themselves and contribute their ideas freely (Sadun, 2022). Moreover, Google's organizational culture promotes a strong sense of mission and purpose. Employees are encouraged to work on projects that they are passionate about and are given the freedom to explore their interests. This approach not only fuels intrinsic motivation but also instills a sense of ownership and responsibility among employees, leading to higher levels of engagement and commitment. Furthermore, Google's culture places a high value on collaboration and teamwork. The company recognizes that innovation often arises from collective efforts and, as a result, it promotes cross-functional collaboration and knowledge-sharing. Employees are encouraged to engage in open discussions, share their expertise, and collaborate across different teams and departments. This collaborative culture fosters a sense of unity and encourages employees to work together towards shared goals, enhancing productivity and fostering a positive work environment (Sadun, 2022).

The impact of Google's organizational culture is evident in the behavior and attitudes of its employees. The company's emphasis on creative thinking and autonomy encourages employees to think outside the box and take calculated risks. It cultivates a mindset of continuous learning and improvement, where employees are not afraid to experiment and learn from failures. This culture of innovation and openness has played a crucial role in Google's success, enabling it to consistently develop groundbreaking products and services (Davenport et al., 2010; Isac et al., 2021; Turner, 2009).

Human resource research can examine the impact of different cultural elements, such as values, norms, and communication styles on employee engagement and productivity. By understanding the cultural dynamics within an organization, human resource research can help identify areas for improvement, foster a positive work environment, and enhance employee satisfaction.

Leadership Styles

Effective leadership plays a crucial role in shaping workforce dynamics. An example that exemplifies the impact of effective leadership on workforce dynamics is the transformational leadership of Elon Musk, the CEO of Tesla and SpaceX.

Musk's leadership style and approach have had a profound influence on shaping the behavior, attitudes, and overall dynamics within these organizations. Musk is known for his visionary thinking, ambition, and relentless pursuit of innovation. He sets audacious goals and challenges the status quo, inspiring his employees to think big and push their limits. His ability to articulate a compelling vision and rally his teams around it has fueled a sense of purpose and dedication among employees. As a transformational leader, Musk leads by example and actively engages with his employees. He is known for his hands-on approach, working alongside his teams and immersing himself in the details of the projects. This hands-on involvement not only fosters a sense of trust and collaboration but also motivates employees to perform at their best.

Musk's leadership style encourages risk-taking and embraces failure as a learning opportunity. He has been quoted as saying, "Failure is an option here. If things are not failing, you are not innovating enough." This mindset creates a culture of experimentation and resilience, where employees are empowered to take calculated risks and think creatively. It promotes a growth mindset and encourages employees to continuously seek improvement and embrace new challenges (Khan, 2021). Additionally, Musk's leadership style emphasizes open communication and transparency. He maintains an active presence on social media platforms, providing updates, sharing insights, and responding to both praise and criticism. This transparent approach fosters a culture of trust, where employees feel valued and included in the decision-making process. It also encourages open dialogue, enabling constructive feedback and the exchange of ideas.

The impact of Musk's effective leadership on workforce dynamics is evident in the achievements of Tesla and SpaceX (Khan, 2021; Snyder, 2018; Williams, 2018). Both companies have made significant advancements in their respective industries, disrupting traditional norms and pushing the boundaries of innovation. The dedication, motivation, and passion exhibited by employees reflect the influence of Musk's leadership style on shaping a high-performance culture (Craig & Amernic, 2020).

Another example that showcases the impact of effective leadership on workforce dynamics is the leadership of Satya Nadella, the CEO of Microsoft. Nadella's leadership style and strategic vision have played a pivotal role in transforming Microsoft's culture and driving its success in the technology industry. When Nadella took over as CEO in 2014, Microsoft was facing challenges in adapting to the rapidly evolving technology landscape.

Nadella's leadership emphasized the importance of fostering a growth mindset and embracing a culture of learning and innovation. He recognized the need for Microsoft to shift from a traditional software-focused company to a more agile and customer-centric organization. His approach to leadership prioritizes empathy and inclusivity. He encourages open and transparent communication, creating an environment where employees feel heard, valued, and empowered. By fostering a sense of psychological safety, he has built a culture that encourages collaboration, risk-taking, and creativity. This has resulted in increased employee engagement and productivity.

Moreover, Nadella's strategic vision has been instrumental in repositioning Microsoft as a leader in cloud computing. He recognized the potential of the cloud and spearheaded the development of Microsoft Azure, a robust cloud platform. This strategic shift not only transformed Microsoft's business model but also created new opportunities for employees to work on cutting-edge technologies and collaborate with customers across other industries. Nadella also championed diversity and inclusion within Microsoft. He believes that diverse teams drive innovation and better represent the diverse customer base they serve. Under his leadership, Microsoft has made significant progress in increasing the representation of women and underrepresented minorities in its workforce and leadership positions (Prakash et al., 2021).

This commitment to diversity and inclusion has enhanced the company's ability to attract top talent and foster a culture of belonging. The impact of Nadella's effective leadership on Microsoft's workforce dynamics is evident in the company's financial performance and industry recognition. During his tenure, Microsoft's market value has more than tripled, and it has regained its position as one of the world's most valuable companies. The company's employee satisfaction and engagement scores have also shown improvement, indicating the positive impact of Nadella's leadership style on the workforce.

Human resource research can explore different leadership styles, such as transformational, transactional, and servant leadership, and their impact on employee motivation, performance, and job satisfaction. By studying the effects of leadership styles, organizations can develop leadership development programs and provide training to enhance leadership effectiveness (Archwell & Mason, 2021).

Employee Motivation

Motivated employees, individuals who possess a strong drive and enthusiasm to perform their job responsibilities effectively, are more likely to be engaged, productive, and committed to their work. They are self-motivated, proactive, and take ownership of their work. When employees are motivated, they exhibit higher levels of engagement, productivity, and commitment to their work, which ultimately benefits both the employees themselves and the organization as a whole.

Motivation is a complex psychological concept that is influenced by various factors. One key factor is intrinsic motivation, which refers to an individual's internal desire to engage in an activity or work because they find it personally fulfilling, enjoyable, or rewarding. Intrinsic motivation is driven by factors such as a sense of accomplishment, personal growth, autonomy, and the alignment of work with one's values and interests. When employees are intrinsically motivated, they are more likely to approach their work with enthusiasm and dedication. They are driven by a genuine passion for what they do, resulting in higher levels of engagement. Motivated employees often go above and beyond their assigned tasks, seek opportunities for learning and development, and take the initiative to contribute innovative ideas and solutions to the organization.

On the other hand, extrinsic motivation also plays a role in driving employee motivation. Extrinsic motivation refers to external factors that influence behavior, such as rewards, recognition, and incentives. While extrinsic motivation can be effective in the short term, it is important to note that sustainable motivation and engagement are primarily fueled by intrinsic factors.

Organizations can foster employee motivation through various strategies. Firstly, providing employees with meaningful work and opportunities for autonomy can enhance their sense of purpose and satisfaction. Allowing employees to have a degree of control and decision-making power in their work enables them to feel valued and respected, which increases their motivation levels. Additionally, recognizing and rewarding employees for their efforts and achievements is crucial in maintaining motivation. This can be in the form of monetary rewards, promotions, public acknowledgments, or even simple acts of appreciation and feedback. Recognizing employees' contributions reinforces their sense of accomplishment and encourages continued engagement and productivity.

Organizations can support the employees' motivation through a positive work environment and a culture that values the employees' well-being. When employees feel supported, respected, and psychologically safe, they are more likely to feel motivated and committed to their work. Providing opportunities for growth and development, such as training programs, career advancement prospects, and challenging assignments, also contributes to employee motivation by fostering a sense of progress and personal fulfillment.

The story of Google's "20% Time" policy is a famous example that highlights the impact of employee motivation. In the early years of the company, Google allowed its employees to dedicate 20% of their work time to pursue personal projects of their choosing, as long as it had the potential to benefit the company in some way. This policy was designed to foster intrinsic motivation by providing employees with autonomy and the opportunity to work on projects they were passionate about. As a result of this policy, many innovative and successful projects emerged, including Gmail, Google News, and Google AdSense.

The 20% Time policy not only allowed employees to pursue their interests and tap into their intrinsic motivation, but it also created a culture of creativity and innovation within the organization. Employees felt empowered, valued, and motivated to contribute their best ideas and efforts (Agnihotri & Bhattacharya, 2022). This example illustrates how intrinsic motivation can drive employees to go above and beyond their assigned tasks. By giving employees the freedom to pursue their passions and interests, organizations can tap into their employees' intrinsic motivation and unlock their full potential. It also emphasizes the importance of providing meaningful work and opportunities for autonomy, as these factors contribute to a sense of purpose and satisfaction among employees.

Human resource research can investigate the factors that influence employee motivation, such as recognition and rewards, career development opportunities, and meaningful work assignments. Through surveys, interviews, and assessments, human resource research can help organizations design motivational strategies and initiatives that align with employees' needs and aspirations.

Teamwork and Collaboration

Effective teamwork and collaboration are essential for achieving organizational goals and fostering a positive work environment. It involves collaboration, communication, and the collective efforts of individuals working towards a common objective. When teams work well together, they can leverage the diverse skills, perspectives, and experiences of their members to overcome challenges, generate innovative solutions, and drive success.

In 1970, the Apollo 13 spacecraft encountered a critical failure during its mission to the moon. The lives of the astronauts were at stake, and it required a collaborative and coordinated effort from multiple teams at NASA to bring them safely back to Earth. Throughout the crisis, teams of engineers, scientists, and astronauts worked together under immense pressure and time constraints. They had to rapidly analyze the situation, devise solutions, and communicate effectively to implement the necessary actions. The success of the mission was largely attributed to the cohesive teamwork, coordination, and mutual trust among the teams involved (Carson et al., 2007; Carter et al., 2015). This example illustrates how effective teamwork can overcome complex challenges and achieve extraordinary outcomes.

In organizations, effective teamwork has several benefits. Firstly, it promotes synergy, where the combined efforts of team members produce results that are greater than the sum of individual contributions. By pooling together their diverse skills, knowledge, and perspectives, teams can generate innovative ideas, make informed decisions, and solve complex problems more effectively.

A more recent real-life example that highlights the importance of effective teamwork and collaboration is the development and distribution of COVID-19 vaccines worldwide. The global response to the COVID-19 pandemic required collaboration and coordination among various stakeholders, including scientists, researchers, pharmaceutical companies, government agencies, healthcare professionals, logistics providers, and community organizations. The development, testing, production, and distribution of vaccines necessitated the collective efforts of these teams to combat the virus and save lives. Researchers and scientists worked collaboratively to develop effective vaccines in record time (Jit et al., 2021). This involved sharing information, conducting clinical trials, and exchanging expertise across borders. Pharmaceutical companies collaborated with research institutions and regulatory bodies to ensure the safety and efficacy of vaccines.

Once the vaccines were approved, teams engaged in extensive logistical planning to manufacture, transport, and distribute the vaccines to millions of people worldwide. This required coordination between manufacturers, transportation companies, healthcare providers, and government agencies to ensure the efficient and equitable distribution of the vaccines. Hence, this example demonstrates how effective teamwork and collaboration can lead to significant societal impact. By leveraging the collective expertise, resources, and efforts of multiple teams, it was possible to develop and distribute vaccines at an unprecedented pace, ultimately saving lives and mitigating the impact of the pandemic (Druedahl et al., 2021; Kucharski et al., 2021).

Human resource research can explore factors that contribute to successful teamwork, including communication, trust, diversity, and shared goals. By studying team dynamics and identifying potential barriers to collaboration, organizations can implement strategies to improve team effectiveness and create a collaborative culture.

Diversity and Inclusion

Diversity and inclusion have become increasingly important in today's organizations. Diversity refers to the range of visible and non-visible characteristics that individuals bring to the workplace, such as gender, age, race, ethnicity, sexual orientation, disability, and cultural background. Inclusion, on the other hand, involves creating a work environment where all employees feel respected, valued, and supported, and have equal opportunities to contribute and succeed.

One real-life example that highlights the importance of diversity and inclusion in organizations is the case of Airbnb. In 2016, Airbnb faced significant criticism for reports of discrimination and bias against guests based on their race. In response to these issues, the company recognized the need to address diversity and inclusion within their platform and organization. To tackle the problem, Airbnb took several steps to promote diversity and inclusion (Murphy, 2016).

They implemented a comprehensive diversity and belonging strategy that included measures to address bias, promote inclusivity, and ensure equal treatment for all users of their platform. One of their key initiatives was the creation of a team dedicated to combating discrimination and bias, known as the "Anti-Discrimination Team." Airbnb also launched the Open Doors initiative, which aims to promote inclusive practices and combat discrimination in the rental marketplace. This initiative included implementing stricter nondiscrimination policies for hosts, providing training and education on unconscious bias, and introducing tools and features that promote fairness and equal treatment.

In addition to their external efforts, Airbnb recognized the importance of diversity and inclusion within their own workforce. They set diversity goals and established programs to increase the representation of underrepresented groups, including women and minorities, at all levels of the organization. They also implemented unconscious bias training for employees and worked towards creating a more inclusive and equitable work environment.

The impact of Airbnb's diversity and inclusion initiatives has been significant. The company reported improvements in guest satisfaction and host retention rates following the implementation of their anti-discrimination measures. They also saw an increase in the number of diverse hosts and guests using their platform, indicating that their efforts were resonating with users who valued inclusive and welcoming experiences (MacInnes et al., 2021).

The case of Airbnb demonstrates that addressing diversity and inclusion is not only a matter of social responsibility but also a strategic business imperative. By proactively tackling issues of discrimination and bias, Airbnb was able to enhance the trust and confidence of their users, attract a diverse user base, and improve their overall brand reputation.

Diversity and inclusion are integral components of human resource research as they focus on creating a more equitable and inclusive work environment that values and embraces individual differences. Human resource research can investigate the impact of diversity in terms of demographics, perspectives, and experiences on workforce dynamics. Research can identify best practices for creating inclusive environments where employees feel valued, respected, and empowered to contribute their unique talents. Human resource research can also help organizations develop diversity and inclusion initiatives, training programs, and policies to foster a diverse and inclusive workforce.

Training and Development

Continuous learning and development are essential for employee growth and organizational success. Investing in training and development programs enables employees to acquire new skills, enhance their knowledge, and improve their performance in their current roles. It empowers them to take on new challenges, expand their capabilities, and contribute more effectively to organizational goals (Ozkeser, 2019).

By providing employees with opportunities for growth and development, organizations not only enhance individual performance but also foster a culture of continuous improvement and professional advancement. Toyota, a renowned automobile manufacturer, places a strong emphasis on training and development as a fundamental part of its corporate culture. The company is committed to developing its employees' skills, knowledge, and abilities to ensure high-quality production and innovation.

One notable program within Toyota is the Toyota Technical Skills Academy. This academy offers comprehensive training programs that focus on technical skills development for employees working on the assembly line, maintenance, and other critical areas. The training covers various aspects, including lean manufacturing principles, quality control methods, problem-solving techniques, and safety protocols. The company also values continuous improvement and encourages employee participation through its widely recognized system called "Kaizen." Kaizen promotes a culture of continuous learning and improvement by encouraging employees at all levels to contribute their ideas, suggestions, and solutions to enhance efficiency, productivity, and quality.

Through this system, employees receive training and guidance on problem-solving methodologies and tools, empowering them to actively participate in the continuous improvement process (Flug et al., 2022). Toyota's commitment to training and development is evident in the company's reputation for quality and efficiency. By investing in employee development, Toyota ensures that its workforce is equipped with the necessary skills and knowledge to consistently produce high-quality vehicles and meet customer expectations.

For the workforce dynamics factor, human resource research can examine the effectiveness of training programs, identify skill gaps, and assess the impact of professional development initiatives on employee performance. By understanding the training needs and preferences of employees, organizations can tailor their training programs to enhance workforce skills, knowledge, and capabilities.

Socio-economic Environment

International conventions and agreements play a significant role in shaping the socio-economic environment by establishing standards, regulations, and guidelines that affect labor markets, trade policies, and social welfare systems. The agreements aim to promote fair and inclusive economic practices, protect workers' rights, and ensure sustainable development. The International Labor Organization (ILO) sets labor standards and promotes decent work for all, addressing issues such as freedom of association, collective bargaining, non-discrimination, and child labor (Thomas & Turnbull, 2021).

The conventions influence workforce dynamics by providing a framework for labor rights, fair employment practices, and social protection. Countries that ratify these conventions are expected to align their labor laws and policies with the principles outlined in the agreements. In the context of economic conditions, international conventions and agreements can influence workforce dynamics by promoting economic stability, reducing inequality, and fostering sustainable development. For instance, agreements such as the United Nations Sustainable Development Goals (SDGs) and the Paris Agreement on climate change advocate for inclusive growth, environmental sustainability, and the transition to a low-carbon economy (Mukhi & Quental, 2019).

These agreements shape the socio-economic environment by encouraging organizations to adopt sustainable practices, invest in renewable energy, and create green jobs. This, in turn, affects workforce dynamics as employees need to acquire new skills and adapt to changing job requirements in the emerging green sectors.

Market trends, influenced by international conventions and agreements, also shape workforce dynamics. Global trade agreements, such as those facilitated by the World Trade Organization (WTO), impact labor markets by influencing the flow of goods, services, and investments across borders. These agreements can lead to shifts in production, changes in job availability, and the need for workforce adjustment. Organizations operating in industries affected by trade agreements may experience changes in demand for specific skills, market competition, and employment patterns.

Workforce dynamics are influenced as employees need to adapt to new market conditions, potentially requiring upskilling or reskilling to remain employable in evolving industries (Laget et al., 2020). Moreover, societal changes influenced by international conventions and agreements also impact workforce dynamics. Conventions on human rights, gender equality, and social inclusion shape the socio-economic environment by advocating for fair treatment, equal opportunities, and diversity. Organizations are expected to comply with these standards and promote inclusivity within their workforce (Wettstein et al., 2019). This may involve implementing policies to address discrimination, creating diversity and inclusion initiatives, and providing equal opportunities for career advancement. These changes in societal norms and expectations influence workforce dynamics by fostering a more inclusive work environment and promoting employee engagement and well-being.

An example of the influence of the socio-economic environment on workforce dynamics in the EU is the impact of the global financial crisis of 2008. Following the financial crisis, many countries in the EU experienced a period of economic downturn, high unemployment rates, and austerity measures. These economic conditions had a direct impact on workforce dynamics, as organizations faced challenges such as downsizing, restructuring, and cost-cutting measures. Employees experienced heightened job insecurity and a shift in their attitudes and behaviors due to economic uncertainty (Isaksen, 2019).

This example highlights how economic conditions can significantly influence workforce dynamics, including employee motivation, job satisfaction, and overall engagement. In addition to economic conditions, market trends also shape workforce dynamics within the EU. Rapid technological advancements, globalization, and shifting consumer preferences have brought about significant changes in various industries (Sima et al., 2020). For instance, the rise of digitalization and automation has transformed the way businesses operate, leading to changes in job roles, skill requirements, and work processes.

Organizations need to adapt to these market trends by upskilling or reskilling their workforce to remain competitive and relevant. This dynamic interaction between market trends and workforce requirements highlights how the socio-economic environment influences the skills, attitudes, and behaviors of employees within the EU.

Societal changes within the EU, such as demographic shifts and evolving cultural norms, also impact workforce dynamics. The EU has been experiencing demographic changes, including an aging population and increasing cultural diversity due to migration (Lutz et al., 2019). These changes bring unique challenges and opportunities for organizations in managing a diverse workforce. Employers must embrace diversity and inclusion initiatives, promote cultural sensitivity, and implement policies that accommodate the needs and preferences of a multicultural workforce. By doing so, organizations can create an inclusive work environment that values individual differences and harnesses the potential of diverse perspectives and talents.

To illustrate the influence of the socio-economic environment on workforce dynamics in the EU, we can consider the ongoing transition towards sustainable and green practices. The EU has placed significant emphasis on sustainability, aiming to transition towards a carbon-neutral and environmentally friendly economy (Montanarella & Panagos, 2021). This shift has led to the emergence of new industries, such as renewable energy and green technologies, while also driving changes in existing sectors. Organizations operating within this socio-economic context need to adapt their workforce strategies to meet the demand for sustainability-focused skills and expertise. This may involve training programs on renewable energy, promoting eco-friendly practices, and aligning business strategies with environmental goals. The societal focus on sustainability and environmental responsibility has thus influenced workforce dynamics, shaping employee behavior, skill requirements, and organizational priorities.

In response to the aforementioned, human resource research can analyze the impact of external factors on employees' attitudes, job satisfaction, and engagement. By monitoring socio-economic trends and conducting research on their impact, organizations can proactively adapt their strategies, policies, and practices to ensure the well-being and success of their workforce.

By considering and effectively managing these workforce dynamics factors, organizations can create a positive work environment that fosters employee engagement, productivity, and overall success. Recognizing the importance of these factors allows organizations to adapt to changing circumstances, promote diversity and inclusion, invest in employee development, and create a supportive culture that attracts and retains top talent. Ultimately, understanding and addressing these factors contributes to a thriving workforce and organizational performance. In this regard, the issues related to workforce dynamics factors that can be evaluated in detail can be summarized as follows:

Organizational Culture

- Values
- Norms
- Communication styles

Leadership Styles

- Transformational
- Transactional
- Servant leadership

Employee Motivation

- Recognition and rewards
- Career development opportunities
- Meaningful work assignments

Teamwork and Collaboration

- Communication
- Trust
- Diversity
- Shared goals

Diversity and Inclusion

- Demographics
- Perspectives
- Experiences

Training and Development

- Skills development
- Continuous learning
- Professional growth

Socio-economic Environment

- Economic conditions
- Market trends
- Societal changes.

In summary, human resource research provides valuable insights into the intricate interplay of factors that shape workforce dynamics within organizations. By examining organizational culture, leadership styles, employee motivation, teamwork, diversity and inclusion, training and development, and the socio-economic environment, human resource research enables organizations to make data-driven decisions and implement strategies that enhance employee engagement, satisfaction, and overall performance.

These factors, including organizational culture, leadership styles, employee motivation, teamwork and collaboration, diversity and inclusion, training and development, and the socio-economic environment, are all interconnected and influence workforce dynamics in unique ways. By understanding and researching these factors, organizations can proactively address challenges and optimize their human capital, ultimately leading to improved organizational outcomes and success.

References

Agnihotri, A., & Bhattacharya, S. (2022). *Google's workplace design for serendipity*. Sage.

Archwell, D., & Mason, J. (2021). Evaluating corporate leadership in the United States: A review of Elon Musk leadership. *African Journal of Emerging Issues, 3*(2), 1–10.

Carson, J. B., Tesluk, P. E., & Marrone, J. A. (2007). Shared leadership in teams: An investigation of antecedent conditions and performance. *Academy of Management Journal, 50*(5), 1217–1234.

Carter, D. R., DeChurch, L. A., Braun, M. T., & Contractor, N. S. (2015). Social network approaches to leadership: An integrative conceptual review. *Journal of Applied Psychology, 100*(3), 597–622.

Craig, R., & Amernic, J. (2020). Benefits and pitfalls of a CEO's personal Twitter messaging. *Strategy & Leadership, 48*(1), 43–48.

Davenport, T. H., Harris, J., & Shapiro, J. (2010). Competing on talent analytics. *Harvard Business Review, 88*(10), 52–58.

Druedahl, L. C., Minssen, T., & Price, W. N. (2021). Collaboration in times of crisis: A study on COVID-19 vaccine R&D partnerships. *Vaccine, 39*(42), 6291–6295.

Flug, J. A., Stellmaker, J. A., Sharpe, R. E., Jr., Jokerst, C. E., Tollefson, C. D., Bowman, A. W., Nordland, M., Hannafin, C. L., & Froemming, A. T. (2022). Kaizen process improvement in radiology: Primer for creating a culture of continuous quality improvement. *RadioGraphics, 42*(3), 919–928.

Isac, N., Dobrin, C., Raphalalani, L. P., & Sonko, M. (2021). Does organizational culture influence job satisfaction? A comparative analysis of two multinational companies. *Revista de Management Comparat International, 22*(2), 138–157.

Isaksen, J. V. (2019). The impact of the financial crisis on European attitudes toward immigration. *Comparative Migration Studies, 7*(1), 1–20.

Jit, M., Ananthakrishnan, A., McKee, M., Wouters, O. J., Beutels, P., & Teerawattananon, Y. (2021). Multi-country collaboration in responding to global infectious disease threats: Lessons for Europe from the COVID-19 pandemic. *The Lancet Regional Health—Europe, 9*, 100221.

Kareem, M. A. (2019). The impact of human resource development on organizational effectiveness: An empirical study. *Management Dynamics in the Knowledge Economy, 7*(1), 29–50.

Khan, M. R. (2021). A critical analysis of Elon Musk's leadership in Tesla motors. *Journal of Global Entrepreneurship Research, 11*(1), 213–222.

Kucharski, A. J., Hodcroft, E. B., & Kraemer, M. U. (2021). Sharing, synthesis and sustainability of data analysis for epidemic preparedness in Europe. *The Lancet Regional Health—Europe, 9*, 100215.

Laget, E., Osnago, A., Rocha, N., & Ruta, M. (2020). Deep trade agreements and global value chains. *Review of Industrial Organization, 57*, 379–410.

Lutz, W., Amran, G., Bélanger, A., Conte, A., Gailey, N., Ghio, D., et al. (2019). *Demographic scenarios for the EU: Migration, population and education*. Publications Office of the European Union.

MacInnes, S., Randle, M., & Dolnicar, S. (2021). Airbnb catering to guests with disabilities—Before, during and after COVID-19. In S. Dolnicar (Ed.), *Airbnb before, during and after COVID-19*. University of Queensland. https://doi.org/10.6084/m9.figshare.14204552

Montanarella, L., & Panagos, P. (2021). The relevance of sustainable soil management within the European Green Deal. *Land Use Policy, 100*, 104950. https://doi.org/10.1016/j.landusepol.2020.104950

Mukhi, U., & Quental, C. (2019). Exploring the challenges and opportunities of the United Nations sustainable development goals: A dialogue between a climate scientist and management scholars. *Corporate Governance: The International Journal of Business in Society, 19*(3), 552–564.

Murphy, L. W. (2016). Airbnb's work to fight discrimination and build inclusion. *Report Submitted to Airbnb, 8*, 2016. Retrieved from https://viagensmerecidas.com.br/wp-content/uploads/2020/06/relatorio-airbnb.pdf

Naveed, R. T., Alhaidan, H., Al Halbusi, H., & Al-Swidi, A. K. (2022). Do organizations really evolve? The critical link between organizational culture and organizational innovation toward organizational effectiveness: Pivotal role of organizational resistance. *Journal of Innovation & Knowledge, 7*(2), 100178.

Ozkeser, B. (2019). Impact of training on employee motivation in human resources management. *Procedia Computer Science, 158*, 802–810.

Prakash, D., Bisla, M., & Rastogi, S. G. (2021). Understanding authentic leadership style: The Satya Nadella Microsoft approach. *Open Journal of Leadership, 10*, 95–109. https://doi.org/10.4236/ojl.2021.1020

Sadun, R. (2022). *Google's secret formula for management? Doing the basics well.* Retrieved April 2023 from https://hbr.org/2017/08/googles-secret-formula-for-management-doing-the-basics-well

Sima, V., Gheorghe, I. G., Subić, J., & Nancu, D. (2020). Influences of the industry 4.0 revolution on the human capital development and consumer behavior: A systematic review. *Sustainability, 12*(10), 4035. https://doi.org/10.3390/su12104035

Sinambela, E. A., Darmawan, D., & Mendrika, V. (2022). Effectiveness of efforts to establish quality human resources in the organization. *Journal of Marketing and Business Research, 2*(1), 47–58.

Snyder, C. B. (2018). *Elon Musk and path-goal theory*. Retrieved from http://sites.psu.edu/leadership/2018/02/18/elon-musk-and-path-goal-theory/

Thomas, H., & Turnbull, P. (2021). From a 'moral commentator' to a 'determined actor'? How the International Labour Organization (ILO) orchestrates the field of international industrial relations. *British Journal of Industrial Relations, 59*(3), 874–898.

Turner, F. (2009). Burning Man at Google: A cultural infrastructure for new media production. *New Media & Society, 11*(1–2), 73–94.

Wettstein, F., Giuliani, E., Santangelo, G. D., & Stahl, G. K. (2019). International business and human rights: A research agenda. *Journal of World Business, 54*(1), 54–65.

Williams, J. (2018). Lesson 6: Contingency and path theories. In *PSYCH 485: Leadership in work settings*. Pennsylvania State University. Retrieved from https://psu.instructure.com/courses/1923777/modules/items/23736221

Chapter 3
Overview of Evaluations

Introduction

Evaluations are conducted for a variety of reasons, such as for management and administrative purposes or for planning and policy purposes, to assess if the project meets the accountability requirements of funding agencies (Chelimsky, 1978). The scope of each evaluation depends on the purposes for which it is being conducted. The other aspects to be considered include how the evaluation questions are asked and the research procedures are conducted. Evaluations cover several related activities, interventions, monitoring of program implementation, and assessment of program utility (Rossi & Freeman, 1982). Evaluation is a systematic and objective assessment of an on-going or completed implementation, its design, implementation and results. The aim is to determine the relevance and response to the objectives, impact and sustainability (Austrian Development Agency, 2009).

Definitions of Evaluation

Evaluation is about understanding, valuing, judging, and making decisions. Preskill and Donaldson (2008) presented the definition of evaluation, as shown in Table 3.1.

From the above definition, Russ-Eft and Preskill (2005) commented that while each definition takes a slightly different view of evaluation, there are some common concepts, such as that evaluation is a system process involving the collection of data regarding questions or issues about society in general, and the organization and program in particular. Furthermore, it is a process of enhancing knowledge and decision-making related to improving the program, process, product or organization, or determining on the continuity or expansion of the program. It means that evaluation should be a process in program development as well as a means of assessment. Evaluation must provide information to enable the designers of programs to continue

N. Kiettikunwong and P. Narot, *Determining Outcomes and Impacts of Human Resource Development Programs*, https://doi.org/10.1007/978-981-97-0395-1_3

Table 3.1 Definition of evaluation

Definition	Distinctive Factors
Evaluation refers to the process of determining the merit, worth or value of things or the product of the process	Oldest definition
The system use of substantive knowledge about the phenomena under investigation and scientific methods to improve it, and to produce knowledge and feedback to determine the worth and significance of evaluands such as education, health, community, and organization programs	Use of knowledge from such as human resources and career development and the application of both qualitative and quantitative methods
Program evaluation is the systematic focus on evaluation as a systematic collection of information about the process that emphasizes the use of activities, characteristics, and the outcomes of evaluation findings of a program to make judgements about improving the effectiveness of the program and/or inform decisions about the future of the program	Focuses on evaluation activities within an organization aiming at organization of learning and development
Evaluative inquiry which is an ongoing process for investigating and understanding the critical issues of an organization	It is an approach to learning what are the organization's integrated work practices, including the organization members' interest and ability in exploring critical issues using evaluation logic and the members' involvement in the evaluation process, and the personal and professional growth of individuals in the organization

to improve and assess programs. A program evaluation provides information for many decisions to improve or stabilize the program at the policy-making level and for administrators to make decisions on collaboration of resources (Preskill, 2004).

The Meaning of Evaluation Research

Evaluation research is a type of social research conducted for evaluative purposes and includes research methodology and assessment processing using special techniques for the evaluation of a social program. Another aspect of evaluation research includes the steps of planning and conducting an evaluation study and the measurement of that evaluation research should enhance knowledge and be usable for decision-making and lead to practical applications (Powell, 2006). Evaluation research is also known as program evaluation. The evaluation is conducted with specific goals using social research methods. Mathison (2004) defined the characteristics of evaluation research as follows: "research evaluation is conducted in the real world and focusses on the outcomes of the process rather than the process itself; evaluation research is employed for design-making purposes, so the goal is to determine whether the process has yielded the desired outcome; it usually represents a middle-ground between pure and applied research and the process employs both qualitative and quantitative research methods. Evaluation research is the systematic application of social research procedures in assessing the conceptualization and design, implementation, and utility of social implementation programs." In other words, evaluation research involves the use social research methodologies to judge and to improve the planning, monitoring, effectiveness, and efficiency of health, education, welfare, and other human service programs (Rossi & Freeman, 1982, p. 20). Moreover, research evaluation can also be classified in various types which generally include:

(1) Formative evaluation: Formative evaluation is known as a baseline study. It involves assessing the needs of the users or target market before embarking on a project. In certain situations, formative evaluation is conducted along the way of the research procedure. Mathison (2004) also pointed out that formative evaluation is the starting point of evaluation research because it sets the tone of the organization's project and provides useful insights for other types of evaluation. Formative evaluation is considered to be a rigorous assessment process to identify potential and actual influences on the program and the effectiveness of the implementation. Formative evaluation can assess whether the program or intervention addresses a need to modify or whether intervention is needed (Stetler et al., 2006).

(2) Mid-term evaluation: Mid-term evaluation entails assessing how far a project has come and determining if it is in line with the set goals and objectives. Mid-term reviews allow an organization to determine if a change or modification of the implementation strategy is necessary, and it also serves for tracking the project.

(3) Summative evaluation: This is known as end-term evaluation or project-completion evaluation and it is conducted immediately after the completion of a project. Here, the researcher examines the value and outputs of the program within the context of the projected results. Summative evaluation allows the organization to measure the degree of success of a project. Such results can be shared with stakeholders, target markets, and prospective investors. The nature of summative evaluation involves realising the overall picture of the program and assessing the overall experience and is conducted at the end of the program. If it concerns learning and instruction, it is the process of assessing the students' knowledge and performance by comparing what the students know with what they should have learned. It is usually conducted at the end of a semester (Müller & Jugdev, 2012; Joyce, 2019).

(4) Outcome evaluation: Outcome evaluation is primarily target-audience oriented because it measures the effects of the project, program, or product on the users. It focuses on providing quick, constructive, and clear feedback on the success of the program. This type of evaluation views the outcomes of the project through the lens of the target audience and it often measures changes such as knowledge-improvement, skill acquisition, and increased job efficiency (Mathison, 2004).

(5) Appreciative inquiry: Appreciative inquiry is a type of evaluation research that pays attention to result-producing approaches. Appreciative Inquiry is commonly called an “asset-based” or “strengths-based” approach to system change. It is based on the concept that when conducting an evaluation scholars, stakeholders, and practitioners should stop focusing on problems in an organization. It reflects the integration of the community of interpretation (Science) and the community of appreciation (Art) by which the organization has resulted in being a unit to be appreciated (Bushe, 2012). In carrying out appreciative inquiry, the research identifies the factors directly responsible for the positive results realized in the course of a project, analyses the reasons for these results, and intensifies the utilization of these factors (Mathison, 2004).

The analytical framework for evaluation is comprised of 10 dimensions identified as: (1) the definition of evaluation, (2) its functions, (3) the objects of evaluation, (4) the variables that should be investigated, (5) the criteria that should be used, (6) the audiences that should be served, (7) the process of doing an evaluation, (8) its methods of inquiry, (9) the characteristics of the evaluator, and (10) the standards that should be used to judge the worth and merit of an evaluation.

The other aspect of evaluation investigated by scholars is evaluation use or utilization. Evaluation utilization is arguably the most used aspect in the area of research evaluation. Johnson et al. (2009) defined evaluation use as the application of the evaluation process, products, or findings to the product or effect. The research team reviewed empirical research on the use of evaluation and categorized studies of evaluation use conducted during the period 1986–2005. Sixty-five empirical studies were included and they can be classified into two categories of factors related to evaluation use: (1) the characteristic of evaluation implementation, and (2) the characteristic of the setting of the policy decision. Each of these categories contained six implementation characteristics: (1) evaluation quality, (2) credibility, (3) relevance, (4) communication quality, (5) findings, and (6) timeliness. There are also six decision or policy setting characteristics: (1) information needs, (2) decision characteristics, (3) political climate, (4) competing information, (5) personal characteristics, and (6) commitment to evaluation. It was pointed out that the most important issues are evaluation quality, decision characteristics, receptiveness to evaluation, findings and relevance. The study also found a new category called stakeholders involvement in facilitating evaluation use and suggested that engagement, interaction, and communication between the evaluation clients and evaluators are also important in the use of evaluations. The stakeholder’s involvement reflects the commitment and receptiveness of evaluation characteristics within the decision and policy setting category. The other new characteristic suggested is an evaluator’s competence.

Table 3.2 Five-step approach to evaluation

Identify the problem	→	If the program's aim is to change people's behavior, you need to be clear what it is you are trying to change and why there is currently a need for this to happen
Review the evidence	→	What you intend to do should be grounded in the evidence of 'what works' and why. Service providers should review the available evidence in order to plan activities which can be expected to achieve the intended behavior change. The evidence should guide what you do and help you to understand the process through which it should work
Draw a logic model	→	A logic model is a diagram which shows, step-by-step, why the activities you plan should achieve your aims. The logic model forms the basis for evaluating the whole project—you are going to test whether these steps happened as planned
Identify indicators and monitor your model	→	Use the logic model to identify indicators (i.e., measurements or observations) that things actually happen as you predicted. You will need to collect data about your project from the start: on inputs, activities, users, short, medium and long-term outcomes
Evaluate logic model	→	Analyze the data you have collected on your various indictors to evaluate how well your project worked for your various users. Report on whether your data suggests the logic model worked as planned. The findings should indicate both the strengths and weaknesses of the program. The results can be used to improve the service

Procedure for Evaluation Activities

The Scottish Government (2016) suggested the Five-step approach to evaluation which can be a guideline for evaluation, as shown in Table 3.2.

Development of Evaluation Methodologies

Evaluation methodologies developed rapidly in the twentieth century (Lay & Papadopoulos, 2007). Guba and Lincoln (1989) submitted that the development of evaluation emerged in the 1900s and can be characterized as measurement oriented. It is also known as the first-generation evaluation. This approach is associated with the scientific management movement in business and industry. It has been used to measure students' progress or to determine the most productive methods of working.

The second wave or second generation of evaluation concentrated on description and led to program evaluations, and the focus on the achievement, strength and weaknesses of the program. It is known as objective-oriented evaluation. Tyler (1980) is an educator who spent eight years evaluating education programs based on the concept that a good program yields the results as stated in the objectives. So, the achievement of an education program is revealed through data collection which reflects the learners' behavior in response to the specified behavioral objectives. These behavioral objectives are evaluated at the end of the study. The report presented by Tyler was widely used for education evaluation during the period 1946–1957. In 1960, evaluation was viewed as an experiment and this was the third generation of evaluation. The process included judgment as an integral part of evaluation. The achievement of the program was based on the concept that the successful program is confirmed by the results of the experiment which respond to the specified objectives. The evaluation is also based on the value and worthiness from judgement based on the obtained data. It was also emphasized that the judgment of a successful project relied on better results when compared with other projects. So, this period of evaluation is also known as judgement-oriented evaluation (Alkin & Ellett, 1990). The fourth generation of evaluation methods (1980–1990) is mainly based on divergent paradigms, known as the constructivist, naturalistic, and interpretative approach. It is the most recent approach in evaluation practice. Lay and Papadopoulos (2007) explained that constructionism is a relativistic stance.

It means that knowledge is viewed as relative to time and place, so there are some doubts about generalization. Lay and Papadopoulos pointed out that this paradigm values subjective meanings. Thus, truth is a matter of consensus among informed and sophisticated constructors, not solely of some correspondence with the objective reality. The fourth-generation evaluation provided more participation from individuals. During this period, new approaches for evaluation emerged such as utilization-focused evaluation, participatory evaluation, and collaboration evaluation. This new paradigm of evaluation was developed in order to be certain that the result of evaluation can be truly utilized for development. The approach considers stakeholders as participants in the evaluation process. The purpose is to establish the sense of belonging and anticipate that the outcomes of the evaluation can be truly useful for future application. It is pointed out that the evaluation during this period is based on the utilization of the outcomes, thus the constructivist methodology is introduced in the evaluation process (Guba & Lincoln, 1989).

The Purposes of Evaluation

Evaluations were widely used in the educational system during the period 1946–1957. After this period, society focused on poverty eradication and the development of industry, the military and education. So, evaluation did not play a vital role in the process. However, in the early 1960s the concept of evaluation was clearly related to experiments and may be known as an experimental evaluation. This concept is based on the idea that the success of the experimental program leads to the specified outcome. The process of evaluation was considered to be a success when it showed a better outcome compared to other programs or gave an equal outcome with less expense (Alkin & Ellett, 1990). During the period 1967–1968 there was a clear movement in evaluation. It was known as judgement-oriented evaluation. This type of evaluation presented the value and worthiness of the program. The evaluation process would provide information for decision-making, whether to change the course or to improve the program.

Based on the first aforementioned process, the evaluation covers the function of evaluation for improvement. Rossi and Freeman (1982) suggested three models under the systematic evaluation process, as follows: (1) Go/no-go decisions whereby the evaluation under this modal is employed to make decisive actions whether or not to impose or establish any functions into the system; (2) Development of a rationale for action. It was pointed out that evaluations sometimes influence the determinants of decisions of the influence parties, such as the political, practical, and resource conditions. Sometimes, evaluation is directly affected by the underlying rationale of a program and consequent professional, political, and legal decisions about it; (3) Legitimation and accountability. Evaluations may serve either program advocates or opponents as inputs into the oversight of programs. This function will provide information on how well interventions are implemented, the extent to which they reach targets, their impacts, and their costs. It was noted that evaluations for legitimation purposes should not be used to justify the status quo with respect to programs. The findings could alert program sponsors and managers and be used as the basis for the modification, expansion, or reduction of interventions (Pankratz & Basten, 2014).

Evaluation Process in Action

When working with human resource development, we usually experience an education project. The education process of evaluation is concerned mainly with the products of learning rather than the process of learning. The main emphasis is on fair and precise scores for individuals, especially in an experimental educational program. The actual process of evaluation must be broadened to include other sources of evidence besides collecting and summarizing the test score of students who have gone through a particular curricular treatment. The results of the course evaluation should be reported based on the searched data and presented as the description of outcomes (Hastings, 1968). The education evaluation process is usually conducted through curriculum and learning outcomes' evaluations. Bloom (1969) described curriculum evaluation as integral parts of classroom instruction which is far from "course improvement". Cronbach (1968) explained that the evaluation process depended on the purpose of such evaluation. So, each purpose calls for somewhat different measurement procedures.

The evaluation process and methods might be modified and expanded for improving educational effectiveness. The outcomes' presentation of the evaluations is required for course or curriculum improvement. Course evaluation should offer what changes of a course's procedures are required and identify aspects of the course that need revision. The outcomes should include: attitude, general understanding, intellectual power, career choices, and aptitude for further learning for a future career. So, techniques such as an interview and essay tests can be conducted among sample groups and the test scores for every student should also be included in the evaluation report. Cronbach commented that evaluation is a fundamental part of curriculum development. The process should be based on evaluation data collection which is obtained from the facts from the outcomes observed. This process of evaluation will provide a deep understanding of the educational process. In a similar situation, the Centers for Disease Control and Prevention (CDC) (Jacenko et al., 2023) presented an evaluation process for health evaluation which is useful for setting a standard for evaluation.

In order to have a better view of the evaluation process, the principles and concepts of research and evaluation can be presented, as shown in Table 3.3.

The detailed functions of the framework for the basic elements of program evaluation via interrelated steps and standards of practice along with the details are presented by MacDonald (2014) as follows:

(1) Engage the stakeholders: The three principal groups of stakeholders should be involved. They are involved in program operations, participation and primary uses.
(2) Describe the program: The details of the program have to be sufficiently described to ensure a shared understanding of the program to be evaluated. The elements include the nature and magnitude of the program's aims to be implemented, the expected effects in terms of what is to be achieved or accomplished, what activities that the program aims to contribute change, the human and financial resources or evidence relevant to the program stage of development context.
(3) Focus on the evaluation design: The clear purpose, the specific persons expected to receive evaluation results for consideration, and the specific way in which information from the evaluation will be applied to meet the purpose of evaluation need identification. It is necessary to define the specific aspects of the program to be evaluated, evaluation methods (cases, mix-methods), questions to be addressed, procedures to protect human subjects, and timeline for implementation or export.
(4) Gather credible evidence: Employ indicators that yield reliable and valid information relevant to the evaluation questions, use multiple resources, and select sources that are explicit to the assessment of the credibility of the evidence, quality and quantity of data or information.

Table 3.3 Principles of research and evaluation

Concept	Research principles	Program evaluation principles
Planning	**Scientific method** • Hypothesis • Data collection • Data analysis • Draw conclusions	**Framework for program evaluation** • Engage stakeholders • Describe the program • Focus on the evaluation design • Gather credible evidence • Justify conclusions • Ensure use and share lessons learned
Decision making	**Investigator-controlled** • Authoritative	**Stakeholder-controlled, participation** • Collaboration
Standards	**Validity** • Internal validity, accuracy • External validity (generalization)	**Repeatability program evaluation standards** • Utility • Feasibility • Propriety • Accuracy
Questions	**Facts** • Descriptions • Association • Effects	**Values** • Quality, merit • Value (worth) • Importance
Design	**Isolate changes and control circumstances** • Experimental influences • Ensure stability over time • Minimize context dependence • Treat contextual factors as the grounding (randomization, statistical control) • Comparison groups are necessary	**Incorporate changes and account for circumstances** • Expand to see all domains of influence • Emphasize flexibility and improvement • Maximize context sensitivity • Consider contextual factors as essential information (hierarchical or ecological modeling) • Comparison groups are optional
Data collection	**Sources** • Limited number • Sampling strategies • Human subjects' protections	**Sources** • Multiple (triangulation check) • Sampling strategies • Human subjects, organizations, and communities' participations • All involved parties

(continued)

Table 3.3 (continued)

Concept	Research principles	Program evaluation principles
Analysis and synthesis	**Timing** • One-time scope (at the end) • Focus on specific variables • Observed outcomes	**Timing** • Ongoing scope (can be both formative and summative) • Integrate all data
Judgement	**Implicit** • Attempt to remain value free	**Explicit** • Examine agreement on values, worthiness, impact factors • State precisely whose values are used

Adapted from: CDC available at http://cdc.gov/eval/guide/introduction/index-htm

(5) Justify conclusion. The framework for conclusions includes five elements: (1) Standards; establish the criteria or norms such as items used to determine whether a program is successful; (2) Analysis, synthesis and interpretation of the findings should be clearly planned and determined before the data collection begins. When disagreement regarding the quality or value of the program emerges, it may indicate that the stakeholders are using different standards as a basis for judgement and provide an opportunity for clarification and negotiation among stakeholders. If the recommendation for action lacks sufficient evidence, it can undermine the credibility of the evaluation. Usually, the judgement for the worth of a program will be based against the standards agreed upon with the stakeholders.

(6) Ensure the use and sharing of lessons learned. Seven elements are to be followed: (1) The design, methods and processes are constructed to achieve the desired needs of the users; (2) Prepare and provide time and opportunity for the primary users to practice how the evaluation findings may be used which will give stakeholders time to explore the positive or negative implications of potential results and identify options for program implementation; (3) Provide feedback by communication to all parties relating to the evaluation. This approach will create trust among stakeholders and keep the work on track; (4) Follow-up. During and after the evaluation, active follow-up with users may be needed to prevent the lessons learned from being overlooked and prevent misuse of information; (5) Communicate the lessons learned from the evaluation to the relevant audiences in an appropriate manner. However, the content of the information should be discussed with stakeholders in advance of dissemination; (6) The release of findings may lead to changes in thinking and practices among individuals in the organization; (7) Standards: The program evaluation standards are classified into five main categories: utility, feasibility, propriety, accuracy, and evaluation accountability.

Conclusion

Evaluation is a broad concept. Evaluations are undertaken to influence the decision, actions and activities of individuals and groups who plan to adjust or modify their actions based on the results of the evaluation effort. The process is useful for decision makers, planners, and involved parties who design social programs to consider if such programs achieve their intended goals. The evaluation process involves both qualitative and quantitative descriptions. The advancement of statistical theory and technical knowledge in the present era have added to the ability of social scientists to carry out the task of evaluation research. The concept of the evaluation process should not be concerned only with products of learning but also the process of learning. Systematic evaluations are invaluable to present and future efforts to improve a development program.

References

Alkin, M. C., & Ellett, F. S., Jr. (1990). Development of evaluation models. In H. J. Walberg & G. D. Haertel (Eds.), *International encyclopedia of educational evaluation* (pp. 15–20). Pergamon Press.

Austrian Development Agency. (2009). *Guidelines for project and program evaluations*. Austria.

Bloom, B. S. (1969). Some theoretical issues relating to educational evaluation. *Teachers College Record, 70*(10), 26–50.

Bushe, G. (2012). Feature choice. Foundations of appreciative inquiry: History, criticism and potential. *AI Practitioner, 14*(1), 1–13.

Chelimsky, E. (1978). Differing perspectives of evaluation. *New Directions for Program Evaluation, 1978*(2), 1–18.

Cronbach, L. J. (1968). Evaluation for course improvement. In N. E. Gronlund (Ed.), *Readings in measurement and evaluation: Education and psychology* (pp. 37–52). Macmillan.

Guba, E. G., & Lincoln, Y. S. (1989). *Fourth generation evaluation*. Sage. Retrieved from http://cdc.gov/eval/guide/introduction/index.htm

Hastings, J. T. (1968). Curriculum evaluation: The why outcomes. In N. E. Gronlund (Ed.), *Readings in measurement and evaluation: Education and psychology* (pp. 53–59). Macmillan.

Jacenko, S., Blough, S., Grant, G., Tohme, R., McFarland, J., Hatcher, C., et al. (2023). Lessons learnt from the applying the Centers for Disease Control and Prevention (CDC) evaluation framework to the measles incident management system response, USA, 2020–2021. *BMJ Global Health, 8*(3), e011861. https://doi.org/10.1136/bmjgh-2023-011861

Johnson, K., Greenseid, L. O., Toal, S. A., King, J. A., Lawrenz, F., & Volkov, B. (2009). Research on evaluation use: A review of the empirical literature from 1986 to 2005. *American Journal of Evaluation, 30*(3), 377–410.

Joyce, A. (2019). *Research method: Formative vs summative evaluation*. Retrieved from https://www.nngroup.com/articles/formative-vs-summative-evaluations/

Lay, M., & Papadopoulos, I. (2007). An exploration of fourth generation evaluation in practice. *Evaluation, 13*(4), 486–495.

MacDonald, G. (2014). *Framework for program evaluation in public health: A checklist of steps and standards*. Retrieved from https://www.wmich.edu/sites/default/files/attachments/u350/2014/CDC_Eval_Framework_Checklist.pdf

Mathison, S. (2004). *Encyclopedia of evaluation*. Sage.

Müller, R., & Jugdev, K. (2012). Critical success factors in projects: Pinto, Slevin, and Prescott—The elucidation of project success. *International Journal of Managing Projects in Business, 5*(4), 575–775.

Pankratz, O., & Basten, D. (2014). Ladder to success—Eliciting project managers' perceptions of IS project success criteria. *International Journal of Information Systems and Project Management, 2*(2), 5–24.

Powell, R. R. (2006). Evaluation research: An overview. *Library Trends, 55*(1), 102–120.

Preskill, H. (2004). *Evaluation models, approaches and design. A handbook on building evaluation capacity* (pp. 102–180). Retrieved from https://www.sagepub.com/sites/default/files/upm-binaries/5068_Preskill_Chapter_5.pdf

Preskill, H., & Donaldson, S. I. (2008). Improving the evidence base for career development programs: Making use of the evaluation profession and positive psychology movement. *Advances in Developing Human Resources, 10*(1), 104–121.

Rossi, P. H., & Freeman, H. E. (1982). *Evaluation: A systematic approach* (2nd ed.). Sage.

Russ-Eft, D., & Preskill, H. (2005). In search of the holy grail: Return on investment evaluation in human resource development. *Advances in Developing Human Resources, 7*(1), 71–85.

Scottish Government. (2016). *Designing and evaluating behavior change interventions*. Retrieved from https://www.gov.scot/publications/5-step-approach-evaluation-designing-evaluating-behaviour-change-interventions/pages/4/

Stetler, C. B., Legro, M. W., Wallace, C. M., Bowman, C., Guihan, M., Hagedorn, H., et al. (2006). The role of formative evaluation in implementation research and the QUERI experience. *Journal of General Internal Medicine, 21*(2), S1–S8.

Tyler, R. W. (1980). Landmarks in the literature: What was learned from the eight-year study. *New York University Education Quarterly, 11*(2), 29–32.

Chapter 4
Concept of Program Evaluation

Introduction

Evaluation is a crucial aspect of various domains. Evaluators strive to assess the effectiveness and outcomes of programs, policies, and interventions. There exists a diverse range of models to systematically analyze and measure the impact of initiatives in different fields, such as education, healthcare, social services, and more. In the field of evaluation, prescriptive models play a significant role in establishing evaluation criteria and identifying key indicators to guide the evaluation process. These models, which have their roots in educational evaluation, provide a structured and systematic approach to evaluating the impact and success of educational initiatives. By employing prescriptive models, evaluators can ensure that evaluations are conducted in a consistent and objective manner, facilitating informed decision-making and driving improvements in educational practices (Gardner, 1977).

Simultaneously, the use of descriptive models has emerged as a valuable approach to understanding and summarizing the underlying causes and characteristics of specific events and phenomena. Descriptive models involve the analysis of historical data to gain insights into the factors that influence program implementation, outcomes, and overall effectiveness. These models provide evaluators with a comprehensive understanding of the complex interplay between various elements involved in program implementation, including goals, resources, leadership, participant characteristics, and external factors. By utilizing descriptive models, evaluators can delve into the intricacies of program dynamics and generate valuable information to inform decision-making and drive improvements. This article explores the significance and application of descriptive models in program evaluation, shedding light on their contributions to enhancing our understanding of program effectiveness and supporting evidence-based decision-making (Dillon, 1998).

By understanding and applying these evaluation models, evaluators can effectively assess the outcomes and impacts of programs, contributing to evidence-based decision-making and program improvement. This chapter explores various program

N. Kiettikunwong and P. Narot, *Determining Outcomes and Impacts of Human Resource Development Programs*, https://doi.org/10.1007/978-981-97-0395-1_4

evaluation models and their appropriate applications, along with the evaluation process. It discusses two types of evaluation models: descriptive models which aim to describe situations and may include expected outcomes, and prescriptive models which provide guidelines and rules for practical use (Stufflebeam & Shinkfield, 2007).

Models for Evaluation

Program evaluation seeks to assess the effects and outcomes of various interventions, policies, practices, services, or innovations, while also exploring how and why these programs work. It encompasses both research study and outcome analysis, employing a systematic approach. The evaluation process draws on various theories, including evaluation theory and program logic modeling (Metcalfe et al., 2008).

A comprehensive program evaluation covers aspects such as causal models, outputs, outcomes, impacts, types of effects studied, effectiveness, efficiency, unintended effects, and qualitative monitoring and assessment of policy programs. It encompasses both formative evaluation (assessing program development and improvement) and summative evaluation (assessing program effectiveness and impact) (Bisang & Zimmermann, 2006).

The primary objectives of program evaluation are to assist in disseminating findings, aid decision-makers in making effective choices, and identify the strengths and weaknesses of projects (Tan et al., 2010). Two types of models are commonly used: descriptive models, which aim to describe programs and their outcomes, and prescriptive models, which provide guidelines and rules for program implementation. These evaluation models are further classified into specific categories based on their purposes and focus areas.

Descriptive models involve using historical data to understand the underlying causes of specific events and summarizing the information in a readily understandable format. A renowned example of a descriptive model is the "descriptive model of implementation" based on nine cases presented by Lucas (1978). These nine cases capture various aspects and factors involved in the implementation process. The cases included in the model encompass factors such as program goals, organizational support, resource allocation, communication, leadership, participant characteristics, external environment, implementation strategies, and program outcomes. Each case represents a specific area of consideration that can influence the success or failure of program implementation. Through systematic examination and assessment of each case, evaluators can gain a comprehensive understanding of the implementation process and identify areas that may require improvement or adjustment.

The benefit of this type of model is that evaluators can gain a detailed and holistic view of implementation by considering multiple dimensions that can impact program outcomes. It helps evaluators and practitioners identify key factors that may influence the success of implementation efforts and guides decision-making throughout the process. By utilizing the descriptive model of implementation, evaluators can effectively analyze and interpret historical data to gain insights into the factors that contribute to successful program implementation. This model provides a structured framework that allows evaluators to identify strengths and weaknesses, assess progress, and make informed decisions based on the findings.

The descriptive model provides insights into past actions and the decision-making process or implementation of policies. An example of a descriptive model is the study conducted by Luthans et al. (1988) on managerial effectiveness. The study employed multiple measures, including a questionnaire completed by subordinates and direct observations, to examine the relationship between day-to-day managerial activities and their effectiveness. The findings of the study assist organizations in identifying the activities and skills required for effective organizational performance (Luthans et al., 1988).

On the other hand, a prescriptive model is an approach that guides data-informed decision-making. It is considered the future of data analysis and aids in decision-making by following four main stages: (1) problem formulation, which involves identifying the nature of the problem and potential decision-making frameworks; (2) finding a solution; (3) conducting post-solution analysis, such as sensitivity analysis; and (4) implementation, which involves executing the chosen solution.

Prescriptive decision analysis integrates normative and descriptive disciplines within decision-making, offering a practical approach to solving real decision problems. It aims to structure and systematize the necessary components for analysis. Brown and Vari (1992) highlighted the significance of descriptive research in informing prescriptive decision guidance, such as addressing cognitive illusions and human limitations through decision aids. Furthermore, prescriptive analysis applies rationality to real-world decision problems, leveraging formal models to enhance understanding and promote the acquisition of accurate information (Riabacke, 2012).

Elangovan (1998) presented a prescriptive model for managerial intervention based on the literature on dispute resolution in various fields. The model incorporates strategies, intervention criteria, and dispute characteristics, utilizing decision-tree logic to guide the intervention process. Key indicators are provided to stakeholders or managers to facilitate decision-making (Elangovan, 1998).

Prescriptive and descriptive evaluation should interact in two ways: (1) descriptive evaluation identifies limitations in human decision-making and challenging decision states, and (2) automated prescriptive systems offer solutions. Prescriptive systems can learn from descriptive research to effectively adapt to changing problem environments. Artificial intelligence (AI) tools can incorporate lessons and procedures derived from descriptive research on human decision-making flexibility. However, it is important to note that while prescriptive models can lack flexibility, expert system models can reproduce the flaws found in human decision makers (Weber & Coskunoglu, 1990).

Types of Evaluation Models

Most evaluation models have their origins in educational evaluation. Biggs (1996), an Australian psychologist, developed a model called the "model of constructive alignment" to evaluate the quality of learning outcomes (Biggs et al., 2001). In 2007, this model was further refined and presented as the 3P model. In the 3P model, P1 represents presage and focuses on factors related to students. This step involves evaluating the knowledge and abilities of learners, which allows instructors to provide appropriate teaching contexts and approaches. The teaching context is also assessed in terms of learning objectives, assessments, the climate or ethos of the institution, and teaching approaches. P2 represents the process and encompasses on-task approaches to learning. P3 represents the product, which refers to the learning outcomes. The evaluation of the constructive alignment model incorporates both qualitative and quantitative measures of achievement (Biggs & Tang, 2007). The constructive mode of teaching, as depicted in Fig. 4.1, illustrates how the model is applied in practice.

In relation to program evaluation, evaluators are tasked with determining the value of a program. In 1972, Scriven (1991) introduced the concept of "goal-free evaluation," where evaluators take on the responsibility of determining which program outcomes to examine, disregarding the program's objectives as a starting point.

When employing such approaches, evaluators should be able to identify the actual accomplishments or non-accomplishments of the program. Scriven justifies this approach based on the extent to which the program meets the identified needs, which are obtained through need assessment. These needs are assessed in terms of their cost to society and the individual. The evaluation focuses on how the program addresses the needs of the client population.

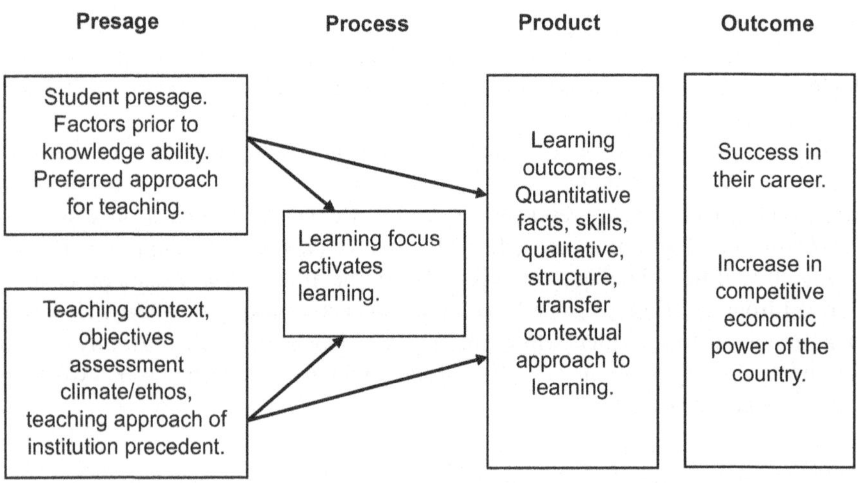

Fig. 4.1 The 3P model of teaching and learning. Adapted from Biggs and Tang (2007)

Fig. 4.2 Alignment of evaluation phases and approaches

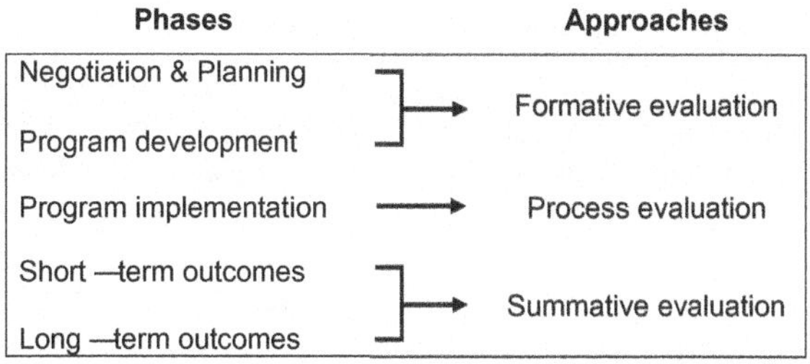

Scriven developed a goal-free model in which evaluators observe without a predefined checklist, accurately record all data, and determine their importance and quality. The evaluator has no preconceived notions about the outcome or goals of the program. The goal-free model aims to provide a description of the program, accurately identify the processes involved, and determine their significance to the program. However, it is important to note that the goal-free model may not be suitable when the evaluator is part of the project.

An example given by Academic Library (2010) illustrates the application of goal-free evaluation. In this scenario, an evaluator might be asked to assess the effectiveness of an adult basic education project within a local adult learning center (ALC) program, which also includes workplace literacy, welfare-to-work, and adult computer literacy projects. Since clients of the ALC may participate in multiple programs, isolating the results of a single project's activities would be challenging. A goal-free evaluation would examine the overall outcomes for the clients of the ALC program, which would provide more meaningful insights than individual evaluations of each project. Thus, Scriven defines evaluation as the process of judging the value and achievements of actions within projects or programs.

Different evaluation approaches are conducted to align with different phases of the program, as suggested by Scriven (1991) and Rossi et al. (1993) (Fig. 4.2).

In contrast, Tyler's (1966) main focus for evaluation is on the specification of objectives and the measurement of outcomes, leading to what is known as objectives-oriented evaluation. This approach involves formulating a statement of educational objectives, classifying them into major types related to students, society, and subject matter, defining and refining each type of objective in terms of behavior, identifying situations where students can display these behaviors, selecting and testing methods for obtaining evidence according to each objective, selecting more promising appraisal methods for further development, and developing the means for interpreting and using the results (Alkin & Christie, 2004, p. 18; Cruickshank, 2018).

Objective-oriented evaluation, as emphasized by Tyler, has had a significant and lasting influence on education, particularly in curriculum design, development, and evaluation. The implementation process involves defining the objectives of learning experiences, identifying learning activities to meet those objectives, organizing the learning environment to achieve the defined objectives, and evaluating and assessing the learning experiences.

Table 4.1 Components of the CIPP model

	Context	Input	Process	Product
Formative orientation	Guidance for choosing goals	Guidance for choosing a program/service strategy	Guidance for implementation	Guidance for decision-making: continuation, modification, or record of achievements
Summative orientation	Record of goals and priorities among record of assessed	Input for specifying the procedural design and reason for their choices	Record the actual process	Record of achievements compared with needs and costs, and back to decisions

Adapted from Stufflebeam (2003)

Another well-known evaluation model is the CIPP (context, input, process, and product) model introduced by Stufflebeam (1983).[1] This model can be applied to various contexts, including administrations, policy boards, funding organizations, and society as a whole. The CIPP model serves as a framework for guiding evaluations of programs, projects, products, institutions, and evaluation systems. According to Stufflebeam (2003, p. 34), evaluation in the scope of the CIPP model is the process of obtaining, providing, and applying descriptive and judgmental information about the merit and worth of an object's goals, design, implementation, and outcomes. It aims to guide improvement decisions, provide accountability reports, inform institution/dissemination decisions, and enhance understanding of the phenomena involved.

The core concepts of the CIPP model are context, input, process, and product evaluation. Context evaluation focuses on assessing problems and opportunities within a defined environment, helping evaluation users to define and assess goals. Input evaluation assesses strategies, work plans, and budgets for the chosen approaches, assisting users in designing improved efforts. Process evaluation involves monitoring, documenting, and assessing activities, aiding users in carrying out improvement efforts. Product evaluation aims to identify and assess both short-term and long-term intended and unintended outcomes (Table 4.1).

Logic Model in Evaluation[2]

The National Health Service (NHS) of the United Kingdom has implemented the Vanguards program, a new care model characterized by national and local implementation with high complexity and uncertainty. To support this approach, the program

[1] More elaboration in Chap. 6.

[2] More elaboration in Chap. 5.

and sites employ a logic model for evaluation. A logic model serves as a snapshot of the program, capturing its components, activities, and expected outcomes.

However, it is important to recognize that a logic model is not a static document but rather a dynamic tool that requires ongoing maintenance and monitoring of outcomes (NHS, 2016). The use of a logic model in evaluation offers several advantages. Firstly, it helps to establish the relationships and assumptions between program activities and desired changes. By clearly outlining the connections between inputs, activities, outputs, and outcomes, a logic model provides a framework for understanding how the program is expected to achieve its intended goals. It also enables evaluators to identify gaps between program components, underlying assumptions, and anticipated outcomes, which can inform the evaluation process and guide decision-making (NHS, 2016).

In practice, it is recommended that a logic model is developed collaboratively with key stakeholders. This collaborative approach fosters a shared understanding and ownership of the program's vision, activities, roles, and responsibilities. By involving stakeholders in the development of the logic model, evaluators can ensure that it accurately reflects their perspectives and expectations. This not only enhances communication and collaboration but also facilitates formative and summative evaluation throughout the program's lifecycle (Hayes et al., 2011; Helitzer et al., 2010).

The benefits of using logic models in evaluation are numerous. Firstly, logic models provide a detailed overview of the program, allowing evaluators and stakeholders to gain a comprehensive understanding of its components and intended outcomes. They also serve as a valuable tool for effective communication, as they provide a shared language and visual representation of the program's logic. Moreover, logic models act as a checking instrument, enabling evaluators to identify gaps, inconsistencies, and potential areas for improvement in the program design. They help to identify key metrics and data requirements, ensuring that the necessary information is collected to evaluate the program's progress and outcomes (NHS, 2016).

Additionally, logic models provide a structured framework for evaluation, promoting a standardized and systematic approach. They focus evaluators' attention on the most important outcomes and activities, enabling them to assess the program's effectiveness and identify areas of success or areas that need improvement. By capturing the logic of the program, logic models help evaluators understand what is working and what is not, allowing for evidence-based decision-making (Hayes et al., 2011).

Furthermore, logic models facilitate learning and knowledge generation. They help evaluators identify key lessons and insights that can be transferred to other programs or initiatives, contributing to the development of an evidence base for effective practice. By highlighting the relationship between program features and outcomes, logic models assist in identifying the critical factors that contribute to program success (NHS, 2016).

It is worth noting that logic models can serve not only as evaluation tools but also as effective planning and project management resources. They provide a roadmap for program implementation and guide decision-making throughout the program's life-cycle. By engaging stakeholders in the logic model development process, it promotes collaboration and shared responsibility among program leaders and members (Hayes et al., 2011).

The Logic Model in Health Development Programs

The Centers for Disease Control and Prevention (CDC) has defined a logic model as a systematic approach to program evaluation, aiming to improve accountability for public health actions. This framework for program evaluation aligns with the CDC's operating principles, which include using science as the basis for decision-making, promoting social equity, functioning effectively as a service agency, prioritizing outcomes, and being accountable (CDC, 1999, p. 1).

The utilization of a logic model in program evaluation enhances the planning and management of activities, ultimately contributing to program effectiveness and accountability. Accountability encompasses various aspects of programs and their evaluations. Program evaluation should be accountable for appropriate resource utilization, effectively addressing the needs of intended users, maintaining comprehensive records, identifying areas for improvement, implementing necessary changes, and aligning processes and results (CDC, 1999, p. 1).

In the evaluation of programs, it is crucial to emphasize practical and ongoing evaluation strategies that involve all program stakeholders, not just the evaluators themselves. The evaluation process aims to summarize and organize the essential elements of program evaluation by: (1) engaging stakeholders; (2) examining program details such as expected outcomes, activities, resources, stages, and logic model; (3) proposing an evaluation design; (4) gathering credible evidence and drawing informed conclusions; (5) analyzing, interpreting, making judgments, and providing recommendations; and (6) sharing lessons learned to provide feedback, follow-up, and dissemination of findings (CDC, 1999, p. 4).

When implementing the logic model, four categories of program evaluation standards are suggested by Koplan et al. (1999). Their framework for program evaluation in public health includes:

1. Utility	To serve the information need for the intended user
2. Feasibility	To be realistic, prudent, diplomatic and frugal
3. Propriety	To behave legally and ethically with regards to the morals of those involved
4. Accuracy	To convey technically accurate information
Standard 1 utility	To ensure that the information needs of evaluation users are sufficient and reliable, and the interpretation of the findings and the clarity and timeliness of the evaluation are carefully managed

(continued)

(continued)

Standard 2 feasibility	To ensure that the evaluation is viable and pragmatic, the procedures should cover practical and nondisruptive procedures and the resources in conducting evaluation should be prudent and contribute to the findings
Standard 3 propriety	To ensure that the evaluation is ethical (concerned for the rights and interests of those involved and affected), the process should develop a protocol and address any agreements for conflicts of interest in a fair manner
Standard 4 accuracy	To ensure that the findings are correct, the process should employ systematic procedures to gather valid and reliable information, apply appropriate qualitative or quantitative methods for the analysis and produce conclusions that are justified outcomes relative to the cost. The overall process usually employs established programs, completes the projects and has them conducted by outside experts

The long-term outcomes of the logic model encompass two key aspects: (1) improved health outcomes resulting from the project; and (2) the recognition of community clinicians as leaders in research projects. The application of the logic model proved beneficial in identifying areas that required further attention, particularly in terms of stakeholders' interests and disseminated activities (Hayes et al., 2011). The program planning process can be visualized and understood through Table 4.2.

Table 4.2 The situation in program evaluation guided by logic modeling

Input		Outputs	Outcomes' impact		
	Activities participation		Short term	Medium	Long-term
Staff	Developed inclusion; Training workshop	Targeted teachers attended	Teachers increased their knowledge of inclusion	Teachers identified appropriate action to take	Improved teaching style
Budget				Teachers implanted effective classroom strategies	Increased classroom success of children with special needs
Partners	Conducted training session		Teachers understand their teaching style		
Research	Provided mentoring		Teachers gained skills through practice in effective teaching strategies		

Cases of Programs' Evaluation

The first case, conducted by Farley-Ripple et al. (2012), delved into the conceptual and methodological issues related to research on the career behavior of school administrators. Their study aimed to examine retention and turnover among K-12 school administrators, employing a quantitative approach for an initial evaluation. By analyzing data obtained from the U.S. Department of Education, specifically focusing on assistant principals and principals in K-12 schools between 1995 and 2009, the researchers explored trends in administrator mobility. They utilized survival analysis to investigate the demographic, professional, and school or district characteristics associated with different types of career moves.

Moving on to the second case, Firestone (2014) explored the topic of teacher evaluation policy and the conflicting theories of motivation. The study encompassed two primary theories: extrinsic incentives, which rely on economic factors to motivate educators and propose different rewards to enhance teaching, and intrinsic incentives, which draw on psychological factors to foster capacity building through training and professional development. Firestone conducted research analysis to identify the policies and practices supported by each theory and discussed the challenges faced by both approaches. The findings indicated that while performance-based pay, such as bonuses or salary increases, may work well in terms of management and labor agreement, it can undermine intrinsic incentives. The study underscored the need for administrators to distribute rewards and sanctions effectively for extrinsic incentives, which require substantial measurement in designing evaluation systems. Moreover, the review of previous research highlighted the growing attention toward combining student improvement data with teaching practice data, emphasizing the importance of understanding the strengths and weaknesses of such approaches. Firestone concluded that a more comprehensive framework for teacher evaluation is needed, alongside professional development opportunities for teachers and administrators.

In the third case, Narot et al. (2008) conducted descriptive research focusing on the manpower planning of educational institutes under the Office of the Non-formal Education Commission, Ministry of Education, Thailand. The study aimed to evaluate the utilization of manpower in these institutes and propose appropriate approaches to enhance their functioning. The research encompassed a survey of 1007 non-formal education centers and a focus group discussion with 160 administrators. Cluster sampling was employed for sample selection, and the study was conducted in four regions of Thailand: North, South, Central, and Northeastern. Additionally, ten expert educators were interviewed to gather insights regarding the directions and qualification requirements for prospective personnel in non-formal education institutes. The research instruments employed included questionnaires for the survey, structural guidelines for the focus group discussion, and a semi-structured interview form. The collected survey data were analyzed descriptively and presented in tabular form, while the information from the focus group discussion and expert interviews underwent content analysis and was reported descriptively. The major findings highlighted the recruitment of various types of personnel, such as government officers, teachers, civil service officers, and government temporary employees, all playing crucial roles in providing educational services. However, it was observed that many personnel were assigned tasks unrelated to their qualifications. The study emphasized the need for improving the quality of non-formal education officers, specifically in terms of teaching adults, understanding adult learning psychology, and arranging community-based education. The evaluation study provided recommendations for a framework to determine qualifications for workforce assignments and suggested appropriate personnel numbers for different sizes of non-formal education centers. Furthermore, the study emphasized the importance of a visionary administrative body capable of adapting to a changing world, developing strategies, and fostering networks to promote lifelong learning among the population.

Lastly, D'Errico et al. (2020) presented an evaluation of connecting national priorities with sustainable development goals (SDGs) in three countries: Finland, Nigeria, and Costa Rica. The evaluation process incorporated a design participation approach that actively involved stakeholders in shaping the evaluation. The guidelines emphasized stakeholder engagement and accountability to citizens by making the evaluation results accessible to the public. Integration and coherence support were the guiding principles for the evaluation, and collaboration with commissioner agencies from various sectors was sought. The study emphasized the meaningful participation of different stakeholders and their contributions to formulating evaluation questions, selecting methodological approaches, and framing the theoretical aspects of the evaluation. By involving all stakeholder groups in planning and analyzing the evaluation, the study aimed to ensure that project benefits were distributed equitably, without undermining the needs and rights of any particular group. The evaluation process followed four main steps of development and design, providing a robust foundation for conducting evaluations that aligned national priorities with SDGs (Fig. 4.3).

The three countries mentioned above are faced with the task of integrating global indicators into their national plans and practices to effectively track progress towards the SDGs. Notably, Finland has taken the lead as the first country to successfully complete the evaluation of its national implementation of the 2030 Agenda (D'Errico et al., 2020).

In Finland, the government entrusted an interdisciplinary team, consisting of representatives from various ministries and research centers, with the responsibility of conducting the evaluation. To ensure a comprehensive evaluation process, the team actively engaged with the international evaluation community, seeking insights and guidance. The evaluation involved the analysis of information, as well as the collection of expert opinions through workshops, interviews, and surveys. Multiple methods, including data collection, surveys, document analysis, stakeholder workshops, and an international evaluation workshop, were employed to gather a wide range of perspectives and insights. The evaluation process received significant participation from the private sector, municipalities, and non-government organizations, emphasizing the collaborative and inclusive nature of the evaluation effort.

Turning to Nigeria, their program, initiated in 2015, is structured into three distinct phases (D'Errico et al., 2020). The first phase involved the establishment of national platforms, which brought together an advisory group comprising representatives

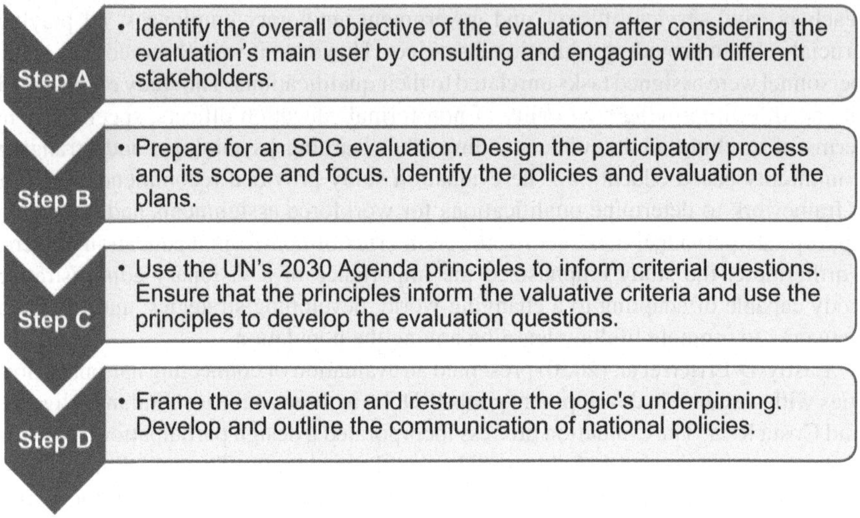

Fig. 4.3 Stages of SDG evaluation preparation

from private and civil society sectors, as well as a donor partner forum. Through extensive consultations with various stakeholders, Nigeria successfully integrated global indicators within its unique national context, ensuring the development of indicators that would inform informed decision-making.

In Costa Rica, the focus is on translating the SDGs into concrete action guided by the 2030 Agenda (D'Errico et al., 2020). Costa Rica adopted a comprehensive approach to evaluation by incorporating evaluations into its National Development Plan (2019–2022), which was complemented by a national evaluation policy. This approach fosters a culture of evaluation by establishing a multi-stakeholder platform that brings together actors from civil society, organizations, government departments, international cooperation agencies, and professional evaluators. This platform facilitates the regular exchange of experiences among participants, leading to the development of joint decisions and fostering collective learning.

From the evaluation experiences of these countries, several lessons can be drawn. Firstly, engaging different stakeholders and involving them in the definition of SDG evaluation objectives is crucial. Secondly, the scope and focus of the evaluation process should be identified through participatory processes, ensuring that all relevant dimensions are considered. Thirdly, the principles underlying the 2030 Agenda should inform the evaluative criteria and evaluation questions. Lastly, the evaluation should encompass the complexity of policies and interventions, employing dynamic plans to effectively communicate findings and engage evaluation users throughout the evaluation process.

It can be said that these cases demonstrate the commitment of countries like Finland, Nigeria, and Costa Rica in aligning their national plans and practices with the SDGs and conducting rigorous evaluations to monitor progress and informed decision-making.

In summary, these four cases demonstrate the breadth and depth of program evaluation research across various contexts and topics. From analyzing career behavior among school administrators to exploring teacher evaluation policies, manpower planning in educational institutes, and the alignment of national priorities with sustainable development goals, each case offers valuable insights into the challenges and opportunities in program evaluation. These studies contribute to the ongoing efforts to improve educational systems, enhance teaching practices, and align policies with broader development goals (Wood, 2001).

The Pivotal Role of Research in Policy

It is widely acknowledged that important policy decisions should be based on evidence. Utilizing high-quality research can offer valuable policy guidance for the U.S. Department of Education's initiative to enhance educational productivity. One proposed approach is to establish a national consortium with two primary objectives: (1) summarizing existing knowledge on educational productivity, efficiency, and cost-effectiveness, and translating academic research into practical implications for policymakers; and (2) developing a research agenda to provide actionable information for educational practice (Baker & Welner, 2012).

Baker and Welner further suggest the creation of a national consortium that would collate reliable productivity information for schools across the nation, drawing upon insights from renowned scholars in the field of educational costs, productivity, and efficiency measurement (see also Kaufman & Watkins, 1996).

The Department of Education can collaborate with experts to establish an agenda encompassing five key factors: (1) enhancing empirical methods and related data; (2) evaluating educational reform models and program strategies; (3) disseminating the evaluation findings; (4) expanding stakeholders' understanding of cost-effectiveness, cost-benefit analysis, and relative efficiency; and (5) supporting the training of future scholars in these research methods. Ensuring that research findings are effectively translated into policy implementation is crucial, with a particular emphasis on the practical implications of research for educational practice.

Evaluation Models, Approaches, and Their Key Characteristics

Preskill and Russ-Eft (2004) provided valuable insights into the various evaluation models and approaches that are commonly utilized in the field. These models and approaches play a crucial role in guiding the evaluation process and informing decision-making. A more elaborate discussion of the characteristics of these models and approaches is outlined in Table 4.3.

Each evaluation model and approach has its own strengths and limitations, making them suitable for different contexts and purposes. Evaluators must carefully select the most appropriate model or approach based on the evaluation's objectives, the program's characteristics, and the needs of stakeholders involved. Preskill and Russ-Eft's (2004) comprehensive overview of these evaluation models and approaches

Table 4.3 Models/approaches and characteristics

Models/approaches	Characteristics
Behavioral objectives	Aims to identify the desired behavioral changes resulting from a program or intervention and uses these objectives as the basis for evaluation. By focusing on observable behaviors, this approach provides a clear framework for evaluating the effectiveness and impact of interventions
The four-level model	Often used to evaluate training and development programs, the four levels of evaluation, developed by Kirkpatrick and Kirkpatrick (2006), are widely utilized. These levels include training outcomes, reactions, learning behaviors, and results. The aim is to investigate the impact of the training on participants at these four levels
Responsive evaluation	The evaluations seek information regarding the needs of the audiences/stakeholders. The findings aim to uncover diverse perspectives on the program and how it is perceived by different individuals
Goal-free evaluation	Focuses on the actual outcomes rather than the intended outcomes of the program. The evaluator has minimal contact with the program managers and staff and is unaware of the program's goals and objectives. The evaluator examines the effects of the program, including any unintended consequences
Utilization-focused evaluation	The stakeholders have a high degree of involvement in many phases of the evaluation. The key question is what the information needs of stakeholders are and how they will utilize the findings. Participatory/collaborative evaluation emphasizes engaging stakeholders in the evaluation process to promote active participation. The stakeholders will utilize the evaluation's findings to inform their decision-making process. The evaluator focuses on identifying the information needs necessary for fostering improvement and self-determination
Organizational learning	The evaluation is perceived as an ongoing activity, with the evaluation issues being shaped and addressed by the organization's members. The evaluation process is seamlessly integrated into the workplace. The central question to be posed is, "What are the information and learning requirements of the individuals, teams, and the organization as a whole?"
Theory-driven evaluation	Focuses on theoretical aspects rather than methodological concerns. The primary objective is to comprehend the program's development and impact. This is accomplished by constructing a preliminary model that outlines how the program is expected to operate

provides evaluators with valuable guidance and options to effectively assess program effectiveness, facilitate learning, and support evidence-based decision-making.

Final Thoughts

Program evaluation serves as a valuable tool for decision makers and policy implementers, assisting them in making informed and effective decisions. Its procedures are designed to provide insights into the performance of a project and the outcomes achieved through interventions. Various approaches and models can be employed to conduct program evaluation.

By conducting evaluations, stakeholders, donors, and citizens have the opportunity to learn about the impact of interventions and identify any barriers encountered. Moreover, evaluations should generate useful knowledge and deliver credible, evidence-based outcomes that empower policy makers, stakeholders, and citizens to make well-informed decisions regarding implemented projects and interventions. It is important to note that evaluation is not intended to assign blame or label individuals or teams; rather, it is about assessing progress, identifying lessons learned for further development, and establishing accountability.

Finally, program evaluation serves as a mechanism for continuous improvement and learning. It enables stakeholders to understand the effectiveness of interventions, identify areas for growth, and make adjustments as necessary. Furthermore, evaluations contribute to the overall transparency and accountability of programs, enhancing trust and confidence among stakeholders and the wider community. Preskill and Russ-Eft's (2004) work sheds light on the significance of evaluation models and approaches, highlighting their role in guiding the evaluation process and facilitating evidence-based decision-making. By embracing evaluation as a constructive and learning-oriented endeavor, decision makers and policy implementers can harness its potential to drive positive change and achieve meaningful outcomes.

References

Academic Library. (2010). *Goal free model*. Retrieved from https://ebrary.net/8293/management/goal-free_model

Alkin, M. C., & Christie, C. A. (2004). An evaluation theory tree. In M. C. Alkin (Ed.), *Evaluation roots: Tracing theorists' views and influences* (pp. 12–65). Sage. Retrieved from http://us.corwin.com/sites/default/files/upm-binaries/5074_Alkin_Chapter_2.pdf

Baker, B., & Welner, K. G. (2012). Evidence and rigor: Scrutinizing the rhetorical embrace of evidence-based decision making. *Educational Researcher, 41*(3), 98–101.

Biggs, J. (1996). Enhancing teaching through constructive alignment. *Higher Education, 32*(3), 347–364.

Biggs, J. B., Kember, D., & Leung, D. Y. P. (2001). The revised two factor study process questionnaire: R-SPQ-2F. *British Journal of Educational Psychology, 71*, 133–149.

Biggs, J. B., & Tang, C. (2007). *Teaching for quality learning at university* (3rd ed.). Society for Research into Higher Education & Open University Press.

Bisang, K., & Zimmermann, W. (2006). Key concepts and methods of programme evaluation and conclusions from forestry practice in Switzerland. *Forest Policy and Economics, 8*(5), 502–511.

Borich, G. D. (1977). Program evaluation: New concepts, new methods. *Focus on Exceptional Children, 9*(3), 1–17.

Brown, R., & Vari, A. (1992). Towards a research agenda for prescriptive decision science: The normative tempered by the descriptive. *Acta Psychologica, 80*(1–3), 33–47.

Centers for Disease Control (CDC). (1999). *Framework for program evaluation* (Morbidity and Mortality Weekly Report) (Vol. 48/No. Re-11). US Department of Health & Human Services. Retrieved from https://www.cdc.gov/mmwr/PDF/rr/rr4811.pdf

Cruickshank, V. (2018). Considering Tyler's curriculum model in health and physical education. *Journal of Education and Educational Development, 5*(1), 207–214.

D'Errico, S., Geoghegan, T., & Piergallini, I. (2020). *Evaluation to connect national priorities with the SDCs: A guide for evaluation commissioners and managers*. International Institute for Environment and Development. Retrieved from https://pubs.iied.org/17739iied

Dillon, S. M. (1998). Descriptive decision making: Comparing theory with practice. In *33rd Annual Operational Research Society of New Zealand Conference* (pp. 99–108). Auckland, New Zealand. Retrieved from https://orsnz.org.nz/conf33/papers/p61.pdf

Elangovan, A. R. (1998). Managerial intervention in organizational disputes: Testing a prescriptive model of strategy selection. *International Journal of Conflict Management, 9*(4), 301–335.

Farley-Ripple, E. N., Solona, D. L., & McDuffie, M. J. (2012). Conceptual and methodological issues in research on school administrator career behavior. *Educational Research, 41*(6), 220–232.

Firestone, W. A. (2014). Teacher evaluation policy and conflicting theories of motivation. *Educational Researcher, 43*(2), 100–107.

Gardner, D. E. (1977). Five evaluation frameworks: Implications for decision making in higher education. *The Journal of Higher Education, 48*(5), 571–593.

Hayes, H., Parchman, M. L., & Howard, R. (2011). A logic model framework for evaluation and planning in a primary care practice-based research network (PBRN). *The Journal of the American Board of Family Medicine, 24*(5), 576–582.

Helitzer, D., Hollis, C., de Hernandez, B. U., Sanders, M., Roybal, S., & Van Deusen, I. (2010). Evaluation for community-based programs: The integration of logic models and factor analysis. *Evaluation and Program Planning, 33*(3), 223–233.

Kaufman, R., & Watkins, R. (1996). Cost-consequences analysis: A case study. *Performance Improvement Quarterly, 7*(1), 87–100. https://doi.org/10.1002/HRDQ.3920070109

Kirkpatrick, D., & Kirkpatrick, J. (2006). *Evaluating training programs: The four levels*. Berrett-Koehler Publishers.

Koplan, J. P., Milstein, R., & Wetterhall, S. (1999). *Framework for program evaluation in public health*. Recommendations and Reports, Framework for 1999; 48 (No. RR-11) (pp. 1–42). MMWR: Centers for Disease Control and Prevention.

Lucas, H. C., Jr. (1978). Empirical evidence for a descriptive model of implementation. *MIS Quarterly, 2*(2), 27–42. Retrieved from https://web.s.ebscohost.com/ehost/pdfviewer/pdfviewer?vid=0&sid=0b2996ac-ff99-4df0-a854-4531ea6f46c4%40redis

Luthans, F., Welsh, D. H., & Taylor III, L. A. (1988). A descriptive model of managerial effectiveness. *Group & Organization Studies, 13*(2), 148–162.

Metcalfe, S. A., Aitken, M. A., & Gaff, C. L. (2008). The importance of program evaluation: How can it be applied to diverse genetics education settings. *Journal of Genetic Counselling, 17*(2), 170–179. https://doi.org/10.1007/s10897-007-913-8

Narot, P., Usaho, C., Rajwijit, J., Waitayachot, Y., & Sakrajai, A. (2008). *Manpower planning of the educational institutes under the Office of Nonformal Education Commission, Permanent Secretary Office, Ministry of Education*. Permanent Secretary Office, Ministry of Education.

National Health Service (NHS). (2016). *Using logic models in evaluation.* Retrieved from https://www.strategyunitwm.nhs.uk/sites/default/files/2017-09/Using%20Logic%20Models%20in%20Evaluation-%20Jul16.pdf

Preskill, H., & Russ-Eft, D. F. (2004). *Building evaluation capacity: Activities for teaching and training.* Sage.

Riabacke, M. (2012). A prescriptive approach to eliciting decision information (Doctoral dissertation, Department of Computer and Systems Sciences, Stockholm University). Retrieved from: http://www.diva-portal.org/smash/get/diva2:516277/FULLTEXT03.pdf

Rossi, P., Freeman, H., & Lipsey, M. (1993). *Evaluation: A systematic approach.* Sage.

Scriven, M. (1991). *Evaluation thesaurus.* Sage.

Stufflebeam, D. L. (1983). The CIPP model for program evaluation. In *Evaluation models* (pp. 117–141). Springer.

Stufflebeam, D. L. (2003). Professional standards and principles for evaluations. *International handbook of educational evaluation*, 279–302.

Stufflebeam, D. J., & Shinkfield, A. J. (2007). *Evaluation theory, models, & applications* (p. 24). Wiley.

Tan, S., Lee, N., & Hall, D. (2010). *CIPP as a model for evaluating spaces.* Retrieved from http://www.swinburne.edu.au/spl/learningspacesproject/

Tyler, R. W. (1966). The objectives and plans for a national assessment of educational progress. *Journal of Educational Measurement, 3*(1), 1–4.

Weber, E. U., & Coskunoglu, O. (1990). Descriptive and prescriptive models of decision-making: Implications for the development of decision aids. IEEE transactions on Systems, *Man, and Cybernetics, 20*(2), 310–317.

Wood, B. B. (2001). Stake's countenance model: Evaluating an environmental education professional development course. *The Journal of Environmental Education, 32*(2), 18–27.

Chapter 5
Implications of the Theory of Change in Program Evaluation

Introduction

In program evaluation, the Theory of Change (ToC) emerges as one of the indispensable tools for comprehending the intricate relationships between actions and outcomes. This theory, rooted in the conviction that an initiative's success hinges on a clearly defined causal pathway, serves as a comprehensive framework that sheds light on the often complex journey from interventions to desired results (Guerzovich et al., 2022). At its essence, ToC transcends the confines of a mere theoretical construct, assuming the role of a practical guide employed by organizations and stakeholders to demystify the "how" and "why" behind the transformative potential of their actions (Stein & Valters, 2012). De Silva et al. (2014) aptly characterize ToC as an elucidation of "how and why an initiative works." It transcends mere speculation, offering a construct open to empirical testing, with rigorous measurement of indicators at each step along the hypothesized causal pathway to impact.

Central to the development of a ToC is its collaborative nature, in which stakeholders with diverse perspectives and expertise engage in its ongoing refinement. As Vogel (2012) observes, ToC evolves and adapts over time to mirror the dynamic nature of interventions and evaluations. This continuous process of reflection is indispensable for grasping change dynamics and their functioning within a program's context. The significance of a ToC transcends its role as a mere conceptual framework; it serves as a robust foundation for monitoring, evaluation, and fostering a culture of continual learning and improvement throughout the entire program cycle. Connell and Kubisch (1998) underscore this pivotal function, emphasizing its role in not only effective program design but also rigorous assessment and continuous enhancement.

This chapter explores how ToC can be leveraged to gain a deeper understanding of the causal relationships underlying program activities and outcomes.

N. Kiettikunwong and P. Narot, *Determining Outcomes and Impacts of Human Resource Development Programs*, https://doi.org/10.1007/978-981-97-0395-1_5

The Fundamental Components of a ToC

As previously discussed, within the domains of program evaluation and strategic planning, the ToC stands as an invaluable framework, providing a structured approach to comprehending the relationship between actions and desired outcomes. ToC is not a mere theoretical abstraction; rather, it serves as a guiding roadmap, systematically illustrating how interventions and activities foster transformation within a specific context (Reinholz & Andrews, 2020).

It involves strategic planning that relies on underlying assumptions to drive change. These assumptions may be grounded in empirical knowledge from experts or research evidence. They serve as a guide for establishing the framework of preconditions and activities that lead to long-term outcomes and input. Additionally, these assumptions provide specific choices and planned activities within a causal pathway, all based on rationales. These assumptions help explain why certain activities are necessary at specific points (Taplin et al., 2013).

Upon closer examination of the foundational underpinnings of a ToC, it becomes evident that this framework comprises various interconnected elements. The two pivotal components that serve as the foundation of a ToC are: **Primary**, a structured logic model that delineates the expected cause-and-effect relationships. **Secondary**, it incorporates a comprehensive understanding of the contextual factors that influence the success or failure of the anticipated change (The Annie E. Casey Foundation, 2022). Based on these two fundamental components of a ToC, it can be further subdivided into the following elements: Inputs/Resources, Activities/Interventions, Outputs, Outcomes, and Assumptions. Figure 5.1 illustrates the grouping and interconnections among each element within the ToC.

Inputs/Resources

This element pertains to the foundational components allocated to an organization or program, serving as the cornerstone of its operational framework and functionality. These resources are diverse and encompass a wide range of assets and support crucial for the program's effectiveness and success. They include resources such as financial support, personnel, equipment, and strategic partnerships allocated to an organization or program.

For example, consider a nonprofit organization dedicated to providing education scholarships to underprivileged students. The program's primary objective is to

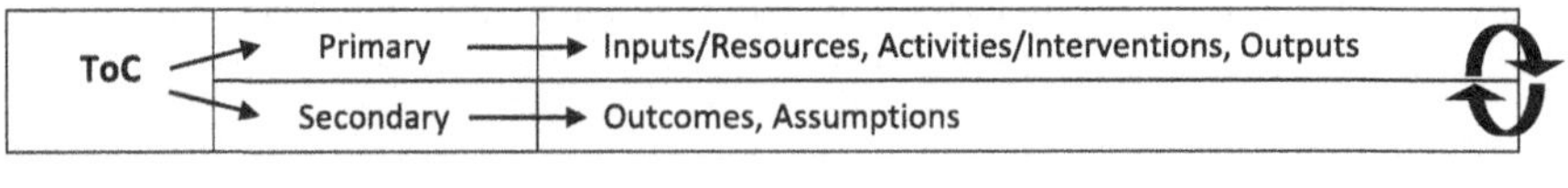

Fig. 5.1 Interconnections of ToC elements

offer financial assistance to students, enabling them to access quality education and improve their future prospects. In this scenario, the financial support acquired by the nonprofit organization is fundamental to its mission. Without sufficient funding, it would be challenging to provide scholarships, pay salaries, and cover essential program costs. The availability of financial resources ensures the sustainability and successful implementation of the program's objective, which, in this case, is to empower underprivileged students with access to education.

In terms of personnel, let us imagine a medical outreach program that aims to provide healthcare services to underserved communities. The medical outreach program relies heavily on a skilled workforce to execute its activities. This workforce includes a diverse range of roles, such as: medical doctors and nurses, program managers, trainers, support staff. As a result, the allocation of personnel in this program is vital for its success (Johnson et al., 2018). Ideally, if a program's success hinges on financial assets, it should prioritize the evaluation or establishment of indicators that align with financial considerations. Conversely, when a program's success relies on the potential and capabilities of its personnel, the human aspect becomes paramount (Breuer et al., 2016). In this context, goal-setting, indicators, and measurement results should be in harmony with the project's critical factors (Chang et al., 2019). The same principle applies to other Inputs/Resources elements as well.

Activities/Interventions

Activities and interventions serve as the dynamic engines powering an organization or program towards the realization of its intended outcomes. These actions are the manifestations of a well-thought-out strategy, and they play a pivotal role in translating a program's mission and objectives into tangible results.

In the context of public health programs, vaccination campaigns represent a critical activity aimed at achieving specific outcomes, such as disease prevention and herd immunity. The World Health Organization's (WHO) global vaccination campaigns provide strong evidence of how well-planned and executed activities result in tangible outcomes. For instance, the "Global Polio Eradication Initiative" led by the WHO and partners involves a structured series of activities, including vaccine distribution, community outreach, and monitoring. Over the years, this program has made substantial progress, reducing polio cases globally, demonstrating how well-designed activities translate into measurable outcomes in the form of disease reduction (Cochi et al., 2016).

In the field of education, well-structured activities and interventions are key to achieving educational objectives. The "Teaching at the Right Level" (TaRL) program, developed by Pratham Education Foundation in India, focuses on customized teaching activities to improve basic math and reading skills among children. Evaluations of the program have consistently shown significant improvements in learning outcomes among students. By tailoring teaching activities to individual learning needs, the program's activities directly lead to improved student performance, demonstrating the link between activities and tangible educational outcomes (Kemmis et al., 2019; Banerji & Chavan, 2020). In summary, activities and interventions are the engines that drive an organization or program towards its intended outcomes. They represent the deliberate, purposeful, and often multifaceted efforts undertaken to address specific issues or challenges. The success of these actions depends on their alignment with the organization's goals, efficient resource utilization, and their ability to create a logical and effective pathway to achieving the desired outcomes.

Outputs

Outputs represent the immediate and direct results that emerge as a direct consequence of the activities and interventions conducted by an organization or program. These results serve as tangible indicators of the work performed and the products or services generated. Therefore, the process of establishing evaluation criteria for this element can be approached from several distinct dimensions (Yang et al., 2023), as outlined below:

Directness and Immediacy of Results—Outputs are the direct outcomes of the activities and interventions conducted. They are often immediate and observable, showcasing the tangible products, services, or changes brought about by the program's actions. For instance, in a healthcare program, the number of vaccines administered, patients treated, or health education sessions conducted represent specific outputs (Breuer et al., 2015).

Tangibility of Deliverables—These outcomes are often tangible and concrete. They can include physical items, services rendered, or clearly defined changes that directly result from the activities. For instance, in an educational program, the number of teaching materials distributed, the hours of training conducted, or the development of educational resources can all represent quantifiable outputs (Taplin et al., 2013).

Quantification and Measurement—Outputs are typically quantifiable and subject to measurement. They provide a clear metric to assess the immediate impact or level of productivity resulting from the program's efforts. Measurement could be in the form of numerical data, such as the quantity of goods produced, the number of individuals reached, or the volume of services provided (Taplin et al., 2013).

Intrinsicness to Program Objectives—These outputs are directly aligned with the objectives and goals of the program. They represent the core deliverables that the program aims to produce. Their measurability and clarity make them critical for

assessing the efficiency and effectiveness of the program's activities in achieving its intended outcomes (Rogers & Weiss, 2007; Jackson, 2013; Pierce et al., 2017).
Progress Indicators—Outputs act as significant indicators of progress. Monitoring and tracking these outputs provide an understanding of the program's advancement toward its goals. Regular assessment of outputs allows for adjustments and improvements to be made, ensuring the program remains on course to achieve its intended outcomes (Berik, 2020).

Outcomes

Outcomes denote the changes, effects, or results that emerge from the activities and outputs of a program or organization. These outcomes are directly linked to the activities conducted and represent the impact or change they have brought about (Nielsen & Randall, 2013). Categorizing outcomes into short-term, intermediate, and long-term outcomes allows for a comprehensive understanding of the duration and significance of the changes observed.

Short-term Outcomes—These outcomes represent immediate changes resulting from the program's activities. They are the initial, direct, and often immediate effects observed as a consequence of the program's interventions. For instance, in a healthcare program, a short-term outcome could be the increased awareness and knowledge about a specific health issue among the targeted population (Breuer et al., 2015).

Intermediate Outcomes—Intermediate outcomes unfold over a slightly longer timeframe, bridging the gap between short-term and long-term changes. These outcomes reflect progress toward achieving broader goals and are often more substantial than short-term outcomes. For example, in an educational program, intermediate outcomes might involve improvements in students' academic performance or changes in their attitudes towards learning (Lawson et al., 2007).

Long-term Outcomes—Long-term outcomes encapsulate the ultimate goals and broader impacts the program aims to achieve. They are the more profound and lasting changes resulting from the cumulative effect of short-term and intermediate outcomes. In an environmental conservation program, a long-term outcome might be the restoration of a particular ecosystem or a substantial reduction in carbon emissions over several years.

By categorizing outcomes into these three temporal categories, programs can better grasp the different levels of change and understand the progression towards their ultimate objectives. Short-term outcomes reflect immediate changes, intermediate outcomes signify progress, and long-term outcomes represent the substantial and enduring impacts (Bauman et al., 2002). Understanding and evaluating these distinct levels of outcomes help in charting the effectiveness and success of the program's efforts over time.

Assumptions

A ToC is not merely a straightforward framework outlining the logical progression from inputs to activities, outputs, and outcomes. It is a complex model that often incorporates assumptions. These assumptions can be explicit, meaning they are clearly stated and acknowledged as part of the theory's design, often based on available evidence or established facts. Alternatively, they can be implicit, not explicitly mentioned in the theory but implicitly understood or accepted as part of the rationale. These assumptions underpin the connections and relationships between these elements, playing a critical role in shaping and guiding the theory's development and implementation (Davies, 2004).

In terms of inputs, assumptions form the foundational rationale that guides the selection of inputs within a ToC. They shape the theory's logic by defining the problem, the expected pathways to solutions, and the envisioned cause-and-effect relationships (Bovaird, 2014). For example, maternal health programs in developing countries often make the assumption that increasing access to skilled healthcare providers during childbirth will lead to a reduction in maternal mortality rates. With this said, the problem at hand is the high maternal mortality rate in the region, which is primarily attributed to a lack of skilled healthcare assistance during childbirth (Thomson et al., 2017). This assumption sets the stage for the ToC, identifying the issue that needs to be addressed. The assumption guides the program to focus on increasing access to skilled healthcare providers as a solution. It suggests that by providing women with access to skilled birth attendants, the risk of maternal mortality will decrease. This becomes the expected pathway to solving the problem. At the cause-and-effect level, the assumption defines the cause-and-effect relationship within the ToC. It establishes the belief that inputs such as training programs for healthcare professionals, the establishment of well-equipped maternal health clinics, and community awareness campaigns will lead to an increase in the availability of skilled healthcare providers.

As a result, this is expected to lead to safer childbirth practices, reduced maternal mortality, and improved maternal health outcomes. In this example, the assumption that increased access to skilled healthcare providers will lead to improved maternal health serves as the foundational rationale for selecting inputs. These inputs might include resources for healthcare training, clinic infrastructure, and community outreach efforts. The assumption shapes the logic of the theory, defining both the problem and the pathway to solutions, and underpins the selection of inputs within the ToC for this maternal health program (Roberton & Sawadogo-Lewis, 2022).

There are also other types of assumptions that underpin the intricate relationships among the core components of the theory, extending beyond just the inputs and encompassing elements outside the scope of the key elements within the framework of

ToC, including activities, outputs, and outcomes. Some examples include contextual assumptions, which recognize that external factors can exert significant influence on the program's success. For instance, a youth development program may assume that socioeconomic conditions within the target community will remain relatively stable, thereby affecting the feasibility of certain activities. People-centric assumptions go beyond the external context and extend to the target population. These assumptions may involve beliefs about the beneficiaries' behaviors, receptiveness, and capacity to engage with the program's activities.

For example, a skills training initiative might assume that participants are motivated to acquire new skills. Rationalizing decision-making assumptions are integral, as the underlying rationale guiding a ToC often finds its expression in these assumptions. This rationale can be based on research, expert knowledge, empirical evidence, or the experience of those involved in program design. Assumptions serve to align the theory with the best available knowledge and practices, grounding it in a rational foundation, among others (Berglund & Leifer, 2017; Zhang-Zhang et al., 2022).

In summary, a ToC can serve as a powerful tool for program planning, implementation, and evaluation. It assists organizations in clarifying their objectives, measuring progress, and adapting to changing circumstances. ToC is often used in conjunction with other evaluation and planning methodologies to provide a comprehensive understanding of how and why a program works. The primary purpose of creating a ToC is to establish a clear and logical framework for comprehending the process by which an organization or program aspires to achieve its goals. In the context of integrating ToC into a human resources development program, the organization typically seeks answers to questions such as whether the program fulfills its objectives, identifies any significant gaps in its interventions (a component addressed within the ToC), recognizes success factors, identifies hindering factors, and determines whether the program is encountering any issues. If issues arise, the ToC can guide strategies to avoid or mitigate them (Stufflebeam, 1998).

In the course of implementing a development program, the objectives usually encompass the enhancement of skills among personnel, obtaining feedback, monitoring outcomes, and evaluating the ultimate goals (Stem et al., 2005). A ToC outlines the expected pathway through which a program or intervention is anticipated to generate specific outcomes or impact. It remains an indispensable tool for program planning, implementation, and evaluation.

Logic Model Based on ToC

For evaluation purposes, it is possible to integrate various models. Concepts from the ToC can be combined with a Logic Model, which is a visual representation or schematic framework that outlines the key components, relationships, and expected outcomes of a program or project in a logical and structured manner. This integration provides an even more comprehensive framework for assessing the impact and effectiveness of a program or project. In practice, the distinction between a ToC and a Logic Model is often not explicitly presented. While a Logic Model typically includes explicit articulation of assumptions and relevant contextual factors of the project, explaining both the 'how' and 'why' of a project, similar to a ToC. From this perspective, a Logic Model can be seen as a different, albeit more structured, format for organizing the same information found in a pathway of change diagram for a ToC (Reinholz & Andrews, 2020). The process of integrating these two models involves aligning the structural elements and core principles of both the ToC and the Logic Model. This integration seeks to unify the depth of understanding provided by the ToC with the precise structuring and detail of the Logic Model. By doing so, it aims to provide a more comprehensive and detailed framework for assessing and evaluating the project's impact and effectiveness. The process of integrating and comprehending both models can be elucidated as follows.

First and foremost, it is essential to grasp the fundamental concepts of both evaluation models. A ToC delineates the program's long-term goals and desired outcomes, along with the underlying assumptions concerning how and why the program will ultimately lead to those outcomes (Allen et al., 2017). Conversely, a Logic Model serves as a visual representation that systematically presents the program's inputs, activities, outputs, as well as short-term, intermediate, and long-term outcomes in either a linear or hierarchical format (Ebenso et al., 2019).

The next step involves the development of a comprehensive ToC. This is achieved by crafting a detailed ToC that explicitly outlines the intended impact of the program, the sequence of changes expected to transpire, and the fundamental assumptions that underlie the program's theory. Following this, it is imperative to specify the long-term outcomes, intermediate outcomes, and short-term outcomes that are integral to the ToC.

Simultaneously, a Logic Model must be created, illustrating the program's inputs (resources), activities (describing how resources are employed), outputs (clearly defining the direct results of activities), and outcomes (indicating short-term, intermediate, and long-term changes). During this stage, it is vital to ensure that the Logic Model aligns seamlessly with the components of the ToC. Each component in the ToC should correspond to an element in the Logic Model (Chen et al., 2018).

The connection between the ToC and the Logic Model is established by recognizing that the ToC serves as the theoretical framework, while the Logic Model provides the practical implementation details. This connection is particularly significant in terms of the short-term, intermediate, and long-term outcomes outlined in the ToC, which must be linked to the corresponding outcomes in the Logic Model. This linkage demonstrates how the program's activities are anticipated to culminate in the desired changes over time.

Subsequently, when it comes to evaluating the program, the evaluators can proceed by assessing whether the Logic Model's inputs, activities, and outputs align with the program's actual implementation. Furthermore, they can evaluate the outcomes at each level (short-term, intermediate, and long-term) to determine if they are being achieved as planned, thus aligning with the ToC. Monitoring, adapting, and learning form the core principles of this evaluation process. Evaluation is essentially a learning process. Evaluators involved in the evaluation program should be prepared to learn and adapt. For instance, as data is collected and the program is evaluated, it may become necessary to modify the Logic Model or the ToC if certain assumptions prove incorrect or if adjustments are needed based on real-world outcomes (Thornton et al., 2017).

The integration of a ToC with a Logic Model yields a structured framework. This framework not only facilitates effective program planning and implementation but also enables a systematic and comprehensive evaluation of the program's impact, taking into account the underlying theories and assumptions. This integration enhances the rigor and depth of program evaluation efforts.

Imagine in the context of improving literacy rates among school children in an underserved community, a nonprofit organization embarks on a strategic initiative. To ensure the efficacy of their literacy program, the organization undertakes the development of a comprehensive Logic Model. This model systematically outlines various facets of the program, commencing with the enumeration of essential inputs, encompassing financial resources, qualified educators, and educational materials. Subsequently, the Logic Model proceeds to expound upon the envisaged activities, which include after-school tutoring sessions and literacy workshops. It further delineates anticipated outputs, quantifying parameters like student participation and the distribution of educational materials. The model culminates with a description of desired outcomes, reflecting the organization's ultimate objectives: the enhancement of reading and comprehension skills among the student demographic.

During the development of this Logic Model, the organization recognizes the need to delve deeper into the underlying rationale and causal pathways that underpin their program. Beyond the 'what' and 'how' components articulated within the Logic Model, the organization acknowledges the necessity to elucidate the 'why.' To attain this deeper understanding, the organization chooses to integrate elements of a ToC into their planning framework (Newton et al., 2013; Reinholz & Andrews, 2020). By incorporating ToC, the organization explicitly articulates a series of underlying assumptions that constitute the foundation of their program.

These assumptions are pivotal to the organization's ToC, representing the fundamental beliefs upon which the success of their program relies. Among these foundational assumptions is the conviction that additional tutoring, combined with access to reading materials, will substantially enhance the literacy rates of the targeted student population. Furthermore, the organization acknowledges the multifaceted influence of the broader community context on the program's success. This encompasses the role of parental involvement, as well as access to socioeconomic and educational resources within the community.

Through the amalgamation of the Logic Model with elements of the ToC, the organization constructs a more holistic and robust framework. This integrated approach not only provides a structured account of 'what' activities are being executed but also elucidates 'why' they are expected to yield favorable outcomes. It introduces rigor and coherence to the underlying assumptions and contextual factors, thereby establishing a comprehensive roadmap for the organization's literacy program. This approach enables stakeholders to not only observe the path the organization is taking but also understand the rationale and anticipated impact underpinning their efforts.

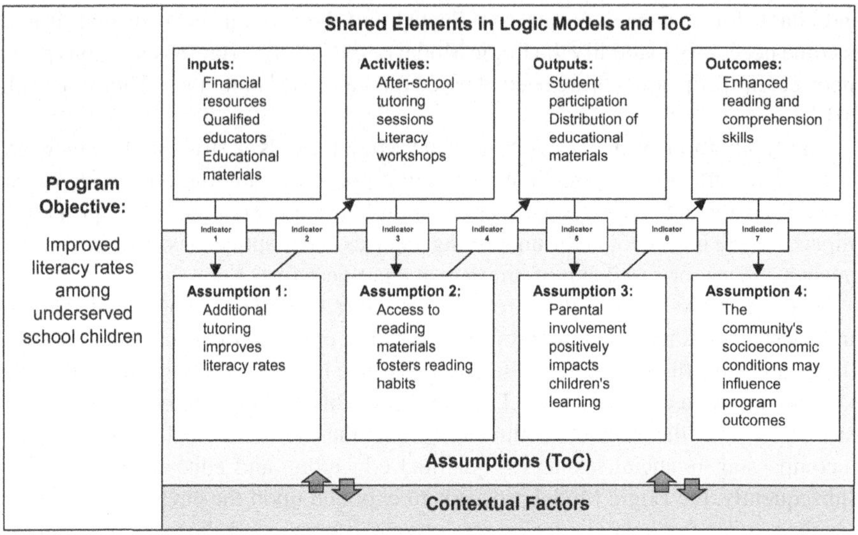

Fig. 5.2 Integrated Logic Model and ToC for literacy program

Figure 5.2 outlines the hypothetical example of integration of the Logic Model and the ToC, providing a structured visualization of the organization's comprehensive framework for the literacy program. It shows not only what activities are conducted but also why they are expected to yield the desired outcomes, supported by underlying assumptions and contextual factors. Additionally, Integrating the ToC and Logic Model approaches can be a potent method for planning and conducting evaluations of programs or projects. Both approaches assist organizations in elucidating their goals, activities, and anticipated outcomes.

Integrated Evaluation Planning Using ToC and Logic Model

The step-by-step guide on how to plan an evaluation using these two approaches together, as outlined in the work by Funnell and Rogers (2011), provides a structured and comprehensive framework for organizations and evaluators to effectively merge the ToC and Logic Model in their evaluation processes. This guide offers a systematic method for conceptualizing, designing, and implementing evaluations that leverage the strengths of both the ToC and Logic Model. It equips stakeholders with the necessary tools to clarify their program objectives, define the logical pathways for achieving them, and determine how to measure progress and success. By following this guide, organizations can enhance the precision and depth of their evaluations, thereby facilitating informed decision-making and fostering continuous program improvement (Lyon & DeSantis, 2010). This comprehensive guide plays a crucial role in bridging the gap between these two essential evaluation tools, allowing evaluators to harness the benefits of each approach while ensuring they work harmoniously to provide a holistic view of program impact and effectiveness.

1. Understanding the Fundamentals: At this phase, it is imperative for the team to ensure a comprehensive grasp of both ToC and Logic Model concepts. While typically utilized independently, these approaches harmonize when integrated. Additionally, engaging stakeholders is vital. In the evaluation process, involving key stakeholders—such as program staff, beneficiaries, funders, and experts—is essential. Their participation in the planning phase is critical for constructing a thorough ToC and Logic Model.
2. Constructing a ToC: The process is initiated by developing a ToC for the program. A ToC serves as a visual representation of the expected program workings, spanning from inputs to impacts. Key steps encompass:

   (1) Identifying the program's long-term goals and desired outcomes.
   (2) Charting the essential preconditions (inputs, activities, outputs) that lead to these outcomes.
   (3) Elucidating the causal pathways and underlying assumptions at each stage.
   (4) Defining indicators to gauge progress at each level of the ToC.

3. Creating a Complementary Logic Model: The organization ensures that it has a well-defined ToC in place. This ToC outlines the long-term outcomes aimed to be achieved and the necessary intermediate outcomes to reach those long-term goals. The organization clearly articulates its strategic objectives, which align with the ultimate outcomes in the ToC. Strategic objectives serve as high-level, overarching goals guiding the organization's work. The next step involves aligning program activities: A review of the organization's programs and projects is conducted to ensure that the activities within them are congruent with the strategic objectives and the intermediate outcomes identified in the ToC. A Logic Model, on the other hand, provides a more linear representation of the evaluation program, showcasing inputs, activities, outputs, and outcomes. Key steps encompass:

   (1) Identifying the available resources (inputs) for the program.
   (2) Describing the activities or interventions to be carried out.
   (3) Specifying outputs.
   (4) Linking the Logic Model to the ToC by aligning elements and illustrating the flow of activities and outcomes.

4. Selection of Evaluation Questions and Indicators: Based on the ToC and Logic Model, the evaluator identifies the evaluation questions to be addressed. These questions should aim to assess whether the program is achieving its intended outcomes. Key Performance Indicators (KPIs) are developed to measure progress toward both the strategic objectives and the intermediate outcomes of the ToC. It is ensured that these KPIs adhere to the SMART criteria: Specific, Measurable, Achievable, Relevant, and Time-bound. If necessary, adjustments are made to

program activities to maintain alignment. In the process of developing outcome measurement questions, the key steps encompass:

(1) Developing specific indicators that will enable progress and success measurement at each stage of the ToC and Logic Model.
(2) Designing Data Collection and Analysis Methods: Determine the data collection methods (e.g., surveys, interviews, observations) to gather data on the identified indicators.
(3) Planning how to analyze the data for assessing program performance and outcomes.

5. Execution of the Evaluation: At this stage, the evaluation is carried out by the evaluator in accordance with the planned approach. Data is collected, analyzed, and the progress and impact of the program are assessed. A robust data collection and monitoring system is implemented to track progress towards the Key Performance Indicators (KPIs) and outcomes. Data is consistently collected, monitored, and analyzed to evaluate whether the programs contribute to the desired outcomes and strategic objectives. When integrating ToC and the Logic Model, it is important to note that iteration and refinement are integral aspects of ToC. The ToC and Logic Model should be revisited and adjusted continuously based on evaluation findings and changing circumstances.
6. Communication and Learning: It is crucial that stakeholders have the opportunity to receive information and understand the program's concept before and after its implementation. Following program implementation and evaluation, evaluators should disseminate the lessons learned from the evaluation within the broader community. These insights should be used to inform future program planning and implementation. Compile the evaluation findings and share them with stakeholders. Utilize the results to make informed decisions regarding program improvement, continuation, or adaptation.

Moreover, the integration not only ensures that program activities closely align with their intended outcomes but also provides a systematic approach for monitoring progress and facilitating continuous improvement. Consequently, these steps maintain a consistent direction for organizational efforts aimed at achieving long-term goals and meaningful impacts. This approach allows organizations to effectively implement strategic alignment within their evaluation processes (Annie, 2004). A comprehensive work plan for the ToC Model, focused on ensuring consistency in the pursuit of long-term goals and meaningful impacts, is presented. This work plan is based on a hypothetical example that seeks to enhance functional literacy[1]

[1] Functional literacy refers to the ability to read, write, and comprehend written material in a way that enables individuals to effectively function in their daily lives. It goes beyond basic reading and writing skills, emphasizing practical applications such as understanding and using written information for tasks like communication, problem-solving, and decision-making in various contexts, including work, family, and community life. In functional literacy, the focus is on practical literacy skills that empower individuals to actively participate in society and achieve their goals.

among housewives in rural communities, empowering them with valuable knowledge for the betterment of their health and families. For more details, please refer to Table 5.1, a hypothetical case of functional literacy program for housewives. Additionally, Table 5.2 illustrates an example of the integration of the ToC and Logic Model in an actual case of professional learning community development, aiming to improve students' scores in the National Test and establish collaborative networks among teachers within the context of Professional Learning Community Development (Maru et al., 2018; Margules et al., 2020).

Table 5.1 depicts the implementation plan of the ToC and Logic Model. A notable strength is the specification of intermediate outcomes, allowing for adaptation and adjustment throughout the program's development process. Next, Table 5.2 demonstrates the integration of the ToC and Logic Model in the establishment of intermediate and ultimate outcomes, using the real case of the Professional Learning Community Development (Narot et al., 2012) as an example.

This case involves the development of collaborative learning among teachers in different schools to enhance their teaching potential, with the expectation that this will ultimately lead to higher National Test scores among local students.

In this case, goals were derived from data collected in gradual stages, known as "the mini steps," which included the analysis of knowledge and behavioral changes of teachers to adjust to the actual situation. The ongoing monitoring and evaluation articulate expected processes and outcomes that can be reviewed over time. This adjustment and learning process was evident during the evaluation, allowing the research team to adapt and revise the plan to align with research goals. The program aims to enhance both teachers' and students' academic capacity through a Professional Learning Community Development initiative. In this context, both the ToC and Logic Model proved to be compatible and valuable tools for revising and adapting the ongoing program, facilitating its progress along the intended pathway and contributing to program improvement. The plan can be presented as shown in Table 5.2.

Final Thoughts on Integrating the ToC

While the ToC is undoubtedly a robust and valuable framework, it, like any tool, is not devoid of weaknesses and limitations. These limitations primarily stem from the complexities and nuances involved in implementing the ToC approach effectively.

One significant limitation of ToC is its potential to oversimplify the intricate nature of social and development programs. The ToC framework necessitates a clear and linear articulation of how inputs lead to desired outcomes, which can inadvertently lead to a reductionist perspective. In reality, social programs often operate in dynamic, complex environments influenced by a multitude of interconnected factors. The ToC may not adequately capture the interplay of these variables, potentially oversimplifying the reality on the ground.

Table 5.1 Application of the ToC and Logic Model in establishing intermediate and ultimate outcomes in a functional literacy program for housewives

Goals	Process			Outcomes		
	Inputs	Activities	Outputs	Short-term	Intermediate	Long-term
• Enhance health awareness among housewives • Improve reading proficiency • Absorb valuable information from reading activities	• Qualified instructors • Educational materials • Learning space • Health resources • Community support • Funding • Technology and internet access • Evaluation tools	• Conducting a needs assessment before the training sessions • Developing supplementary reading materials with nutritional content • Implementing the learning package as required • Offering cooking classes as an active learning approach using the reading materials as a base • Conducting evaluations of outputs and outcomes • Holding evening classes twice a week	• The level of reading literacy increased • Interest in participating in reading and cooking classes increased	• Increased interest in reading and beneficial programs • Willingness to share family experiences • Sharing valuable information • Improved reading abilities	• Enhanced awareness and participation • Knowledge sharing and communication • Dissemination of valuable information • Enhanced literacy skills	• Improved health and family knowledge • Positive attitude towards healthy eating • Enhanced lifestyle through active learning

Table 5.2 Application of the ToC and Logic Model in Logic Model in professional learning community development

Goals	Process			Outcomes		
	Inputs	Activities	Outputs	Short-term	Intermediate	Long-term
• Enhance teaching effectiveness • Increase student academic performance • Foster collaborative networks	• Qualified trainers • Educational materials • Time and training sessions • Assessment tools • Collaborative workshops • Communication and networking resources • Monitoring and evaluation framework	• Identify the basic knowledge and skills • Identify lead teachers • Develop a curriculum • Implement active learning strategies • Employ participatory action research • Conduct pre-post tests • Hold focus group monitoring sessions • Utilize knowledge management as a development tool	• Teachers acquire improved teaching skills • Students demonstrate enhanced analytical thinking skills • Teachers exhibit trust and collaboration with their peers in academic activities	• Teachers effectively apply newly acquired teaching skills • Students actively demonstrate enhanced analytical thinking skills • Teachers actively participate in collaborative pedagogical planning with their peers to enhance teaching strategies and resource sharing	• Increased classroom engagement • Improved academic performance • Collaborative teaching strategies	• The improvement of students' scores on the national test • Teachers establish collaborative networks with other local schools

Furthermore, the effectiveness of a ToC largely depends on the accuracy of the underlying assumptions. If these assumptions are flawed or based on incomplete information, it can lead to inaccurate expectations and misguided program planning. The ToC relies on a certain degree of predictability in the cause-and-effect relationships between inputs, activities, and outcomes. In situations where this predictability is low, such as in highly unpredictable or unstable environments, the ToC's utility may be limited (Davies, 2018).

Another limitation relates to the sometimes rigid structure of the ToC framework. While the linearity of the model can be an advantage for clarity and communication, it can be a drawback when working in contexts where adaptability and flexibility are paramount. In rapidly changing environments, adhering too strictly to a predefined ToC can stifle an organization's ability to respond to unexpected challenges and seize emerging opportunities.

Additionally, there is the risk of confirmation bias[2] in using ToC for program evaluation. When organizations invest significant resources in the development of a ToC, there can be a tendency to focus on confirming its assumptions rather than critically assessing the program's impact. This confirmation bias can hinder objective evaluation and potentially lead to a perpetuation of ineffective programs. Additional weaknesses of ToC can be summarized (Lam, 2020) as follows:

Assumption-Based—ToC relies heavily on assumptions about the causal relationships between program activities and outcomes. If these assumptions are incorrect or not well-supported, the entire ToC can be flawed. In practice, it can be challenging to validate all these assumptions empirically, leading to potential biases and inaccuracies in the evaluation process.

Simplification of Reality—ToC often simplifies complex social and environmental contexts into linear or straightforward cause-and-effect relationships. In reality, these relationships can be much more intricate and non-linear. This oversimplification can lead to a misrepresentation of how change occurs, and it may not adequately account for external factors or unintended consequences.

Lack of Flexibility—ToC is typically developed at the outset of a program and tends to remain relatively static. This lack of flexibility can make it challenging to adapt to changing circumstances, emerging evidence, or new insights gained during program implementation. As a result, ToC may not adequately capture the dynamic nature of many interventions.

[2] A cognitive tendency that describes the human inclination to seek, interpret, and remember information that confirms one's existing beliefs or hypotheses. It leads individuals to favor information that supports their preconceptions while dismissing or ignoring evidence that contradicts their established views. This bias can influence decision-making, leading people to perceive information selectively and reinforce their existing opinions or beliefs, potentially hindering a more objective and comprehensive understanding of a situation or topic.

Limited Predictive Power—ToC is primarily a descriptive tool that helps stakeholders understand and visualize the expected pathways to change. However, it may not serve as a strong predictive tool for precisely forecasting outcomes or quantifying the magnitude of change. It doesn't provide statistical evidence or predictions in the same way that some other evaluation methodologies do.

Resource-Intensive—Developing a comprehensive ToC can be resource-intensive, requiring time, expertise, and data. Smaller organizations or programs with limited resources may find it challenging to create and maintain a ToC, which could limit its accessibility as an evaluation tool.

Subjectivity—Developing a ToC often involves the input of various stakeholders, which can introduce subjectivity and bias. Different stakeholders may have varying perspectives on the causal pathways and assumptions, leading to potential disagreements or inconsistencies in the ToC.

Interpretation and Communication—Effectively communicating the ToC to diverse stakeholders can be challenging. It may necessitate complex diagrams or narratives that not everyone can easily understand, potentially limiting its accessibility and utility as a communication tool.

Finally, the process of developing a ToC can be resource-intensive, both in terms of time and expertise. Smaller organizations or those with limited budgets may find it challenging to engage in the rigorous process of ToC development (Funnell & Rogers, 2011). This limitation can lead to disparities in the adoption of ToC-based evaluation, with well-resourced organizations benefiting more from its advantages. However, despite these weaknesses, the ToC remains a valuable framework for program planning and evaluation when used appropriately and in conjunction with other evaluation methods. Recognizing its limitations and being open to adapting the ToC as needed can help mitigate some of these weaknesses and make it a more effective tool for understanding and assessing the impact of programs and interventions (De Silva et al, 2014).

In summary, the ToC is a versatile tool that can be effectively utilized in both the development and evaluation phases of a program's lifecycle. It assists organizations in articulating their program's logic and goals, which is essential for the successful planning, implementation, and assessment of social and development initiatives. The ToC serves as a valuable framework in program evaluation and planning to elucidate the underlying assumptions and logic governing how a program or intervention is expected to bring about specific outcomes (Dhillon & Vaca, 2018).

References

Allen, W., Cruz, J., & Warburton, B. (2017). How decision support systems can benefit from a theory of change approach. *Environmental Management, 59*, 956–965.

Annie, E. (2004). Theory of change: A practical tool for action, results and learning. *Casey Foundation,* 10–11.

Banerji, R., & Chavan, M. (2020). A twenty-year partnership of practice and research: The Nobel laureates and Pratham in India. *World Development, 127*, 104788.

Bauman, A. E., Sallis, J. F., Dzewaltowski, D. A., & Owen, N. (2002). Toward a better understanding of the influences on physical activity: The role of determinants, correlates, causal variables, mediators, moderators, and confounders. *American Journal of Preventive Medicine, 23*(2), 5–14.

Berglund, A., & Leifer, L. (2017). Beyond design thinking-whose perspective is driving the people-centric approach to change. In *DS 88: Proceedings of the 19th International Conference on Engineering and Product Design Education (E&PDE17), Building Community: Design Education for a Sustainable Future*, Oslo, Norway, September 7 & 8, 2017 (pp. 613–618).

Berik, G. (2020). Measuring what matters and guiding policy: An evaluation of the Genuine Progress Indicator. *International Labour Review, 159*(1), 71–94.

Bovaird, T. (2014). Attributing outcomes to social policy interventions—'Gold standard' or 'fool's gold' in public policy and management? *Social Policy & Administration, 48*(1), 1–23.

Breuer, E., De Silva, M. J., Shidaye, R., Petersen, I., Nakku, J., Jordans, M. J., Fekadu, A., & Lund, C. (2016). Planning and evaluating mental health services in low- and middle-income countries using theory of change. *The British Journal of Psychiatry, 208*(s56), s55–s62.

Breuer, E., Lee, L., De Silva, M., & Lund, C. (2015). Using theory of change to design and evaluate public health interventions: A systematic review. *Implementation Science, 11*, 1–17.

Chang, J. Y., Jiang, J. J., Klein, G., & Wang, E. T. (2019). Enterprise system programs: Goal setting and cooperation in the integration team. *Information & Management, 56*(6), 103137.

Chen, H. T., Pan, H. L. W., Morosanu, L., & Turner, N. (2018). Using logic models and the action model/change model schema in planning the learning community program: A comparative case study. *Canadian Journal of Program Evaluation, 33*(1), 49–68.

Cochi, S. L., Hegg, L., Kaur, A., Pandak, C., & Jafari, H. (2016). The global polio eradication initiative: Progress, lessons learned, and polio legacy transition planning. *Health Affairs, 35*(2), 277–283.

Connell, J. P., & Kubisch, A. C. (1998). Applying a theory of change approach to the evaluation of comprehensive community initiatives: Progress, prospects, and problems. *New Approaches to Evaluating Community Initiatives, 2*(15–44), 1–16.

Davies, R. (2004). Scale, complexity and the representation of theories of change. *Evaluation, 10*(1), 101–121.

Davies, R. (2018). Representing theories of change: Technical challenges with evaluation consequences. *Journal of Development Effectiveness, 10*(4), 438–461.

De Silva, M. J., Breuer, E., Lee, L., Asher, L., Chowdhary, N., Lund, C., & Patel, V. (2014). Theory of change: A theory-driven approach to enhance the Medical Research Council's framework for complex interventions. *Trials, 15*(1), 1–13.

Dhillon, L., & Vaca, S. (2018). Refining theories of change. *Evaluation, 14*(30), 64–87.

Ebenso, B., Manzano, A., Uzochukwu, B., Etiaba, E., Huss, R., Ensor, T., Newell, J., Onwujekwe, O., Ezumah, N., Hicks, J., & Mirzoev, T. (2019). Dealing with context in logic model development: Reflections from a realist evaluation of a community health worker programme in Nigeria. *Evaluation and Program Planning, 73*, 97–110.

Funnell, S. C., & Rogers, P. J. (2011). *Purposeful program theory: Effective use of theories of change and logic models*. Wiley.

Guerzovich, F., Aston, T., Levy, B., Chies Schommer, P., Haines, R., Cant, S., & Faria Zimmer Santos, G. (2022). How do we shape and navigate pathways to social accountability scale? Introducing a middle-level theory of change.

Jackson, E. T. (2013). Interrogating the theory of change: Evaluating impact investing where it matters most. *Journal of Sustainable Finance & Investment, 3*(2), 95–110.

Johnson, G. E., Wright, F. C., & Foster, K. (2018). The impact of rural outreach programs on medical students' future rural intentions and working locations: A systematic review. *BMC Medical Education, 18*, 1–19.

Kemmis, S., McTaggart, R., & Nixon, R. (2019). Critical participatory action research. In *Action learning and action research: Genres and approaches* (pp. 179–192). Emerald Publishing Limited.

Lam, S. (2020). Toward learning from change pathways: Reviewing theory of change and its discontents. *Canadian Journal of Program Evaluation, 35*(2), 188–203.

Lawson, H. A., Claiborne, N., Hardiman, E., Austin, S., & Surko, M. (2007). Deriving theories of change from successful community development partnerships for youths: Implications for school improvement. *American Journal of Education, 114*(1), 1–40.

Lyon, K., & DeSantis, J. (2010). Planning, implementing, and evaluating training projects for public child welfare agency supervisors: The application of logic models and theory of change. *Journal of Child and Youth Care Work, 23*, 147–167.

Margules, C., Boedhihartono, A. K., Langston, J. D., Riggs, R. A., Sari, D. A., Sarkar, S., Sayer, J. A., Supriatna, J., & Winarni, N. L. (2020). Transdisciplinary science for improved conservation outcomes. *Environmental Conservation, 47*(4), 224–233.

Maru, Y. T., Sparrow, A., Butler, J. R., Banerjee, O., Ison, R., Hall, A., & Carberry, P. (2018). Towards appropriate mainstreaming of "theory of change" approaches into agricultural research for development: Challenges and opportunities. *Agricultural Systems, 165*, 344–353.

Narot, P., Trantrirat, S., Arirattana, W., Yuenyoung, C., Hiengrat, C., & Trisirirat, J. (2012). *Local learning enrichment network: Khon Kaen province.* Thailand Research Fund.

Newton, X. A., Poon, R. C., Nunes, N. L., & Stone, E. M. (2013). Research on teacher education programs: Logic model approach. *Evaluation and Program Planning, 36*(1), 88–96.

Nielsen, K., & Randall, R. (2013). Opening the black box: Presenting a model for evaluating organizational-level interventions. *European Journal of Work and Organizational Psychology, 22*(5), 601–617.

Pierce, S., Gould, D., & Camiré, M. (2017). Definition and model of life skills transfer. *International Review of Sport and Exercise Psychology, 10*(1), 186–211.

Reinholz, D. L., & Andrews, T. C. (2020). Change theory and theory of change: What's the difference anyway? *International Journal of STEM Education, 7*(1), 1–12.

Roberton, T., & Sawadogo-Lewis, T. (2022). Building coherent monitoring and evaluation plans with the evaluation planning tool for global health. *Global Health Action, 15*(sup1), 2067396.

Rogers, P. J., & Weiss, C. H. (2007). Theory-based evaluation: Reflections ten years on: Theory-based evaluation: Past, present, and future. *New Directions for Evaluation, 2007*(114), 63–81.

Stein, D., & Valters, C. (2012). *Understanding theory of change in international development: A review of existing knowledge.* Paper prepared for The Asia Foundation and the Justice and Security Research Programme at the London School of Economics and Political Science.

Stem, C., Margoluis, R., Salafsky, N., & Brown, M. (2005). Monitoring and evaluation in conservation: A review of trends and approaches. *Conservation Biology, 19*(2), 295–309.

Stufflebeam, D. L. (1998). Conflicts between standards-based and postmodernist evaluations: Toward rapprochement. *Journal of Personnel Evaluation in Education, 12*, 287–296.

Taplin, D. H., Clark, H., Collins, E., & Colby, D. C. (2013). *Theory of change.* Technical papers: A series of papers to support development of theories of change based on practice in the field. ActKnowledge, New York, NY.

The Annie E. Casey Foundation. (2022). *Developing a theory of change: Practical guidance (Part I).* Retrieved from https://assets.aecf.org/m/resourcedoc/aecf-theoryofchange-guidance-2022.pdf

Thomson, M., Kentikelenis, A., & Stubbs, T. (2017). Structural adjustment programmes adversely affect vulnerable populations: A systematic-narrative review of their effect on child and maternal health. *Public Health Reviews, 38*, 1–18.

Thornton, P. K., Schuetz, T., Förch, W., Cramer, L., Abreu, D., Vermeulen, S., & Campbell, B. M. (2017). Responding to global change: A theory of change approach to making agricultural research for development outcome-based. *Agricultural Systems, 152*, 145–153.

Vogel, I. (2012). *Review of the use of 'theory of change' in international development*. UK Department of International Development. Retrieved September 10, 2021 from https://www.theoryofchange.org/pdf/DFID_ToC_Review_VogelV7.pdf

Yang, Z., Ahmad, S., Bernardi, A., Shang, W. L., Xuan, J., & Xu, B. (2023). Evaluating alternative low carbon fuel technologies using a stakeholder participation-based q-rung orthopair linguistic multi-criteria framework. *Applied Energy, 332*, 120492.

Zhang-Zhang, Y., Rohlfer, S., & Varma, A. (2022). Strategic people management in contemporary highly dynamic VUCA contexts: A knowledge worker perspective. *Journal of Business Research, 144*, 587–598.

Chapter 6
A Critical Examination of Kirkpatrick, Bushnell, Warr et al., and Stufflebeam and Zhang's Evaluation Models

Introduction

To fulfill the ultimate intended purposes of successfully determining the outcomes and impacts of human resource research, it is desirable to understand the interplay between existing evaluative methodologies that ensure the seamless alignment of various HR training programs with organizational goals. Among these methodologies, several distinguished models have emerged as prominent contenders in the field of HR training program evaluation. This chapter embarks on a comprehensive exploration, critique, and comparison of four noteworthy evaluation models: Kirkpatrick (2006), Bushnell (1990), Warr et al. (1970), Stufflebeam and Zhang (2017), among others. The selection of an appropriate evaluation model holds the key to deciphering the strengths and areas of improvement within these programs, which ultimately paves the way for their optimization.

The exploration begins with the classical Kirkpatrick model, pioneered by Donald Kirkpatrick in the 1950s and further developed by his son, James D. Kirkpatrick. This well-established model categorizes evaluation into four hierarchical levels, progressively assessing participant reactions, learning outcomes, behavior changes, and, most critically, the impact on organizational results. The Kirkpatrick model, thus, offers a comprehensive approach to evaluating HR programs.

Next is Bushnell's IPO model (Bushnell, 1990), an approach that focuses on Input, Process, and Output. This model places substantial emphasis on aligning program design and execution with the desired outcomes, thereby accentuating the importance of structuring HR programs for success.

While Warr et al.'s CIRO model delves into the domains of Context, Input, Reaction, and Output and underlines the interplay between program-specific and contextual factors, offering a more nuanced approach to program evaluation by accounting for external influences, Stufflebeam and Zhang's CIPP model (Stufflebeam & Zhang, 2017), which stands for Context, Input, Process, and Product and is notable for its versatility and the depth of analysis it affords in its evaluation approach, integrates

N. Kiettikunwong and P. Narot, *Determining Outcomes and Impacts of Human Resource Development Programs*, https://doi.org/10.1007/978-981-97-0395-1_6

contextual factors, program design, implementation processes, and the achievement of specific products or outcomes.

This comparison utilizes Kirkpatrick's 4-level model as the basis for comparing other models. The objective is to uncover similarities and differences across various dimensions. Ultimately, this chapter aims to offer a comprehensive understanding of the strengths and limitations of each model, aiding HR practitioners and organizational leaders in enhancing their program evaluation methodologies. This endeavor will contribute to the enhancement of HR practices and organizational performance.

The Concept of the Kirkpatrick Evaluation Model

The Kirkpatrick Evaluation Model, introduced by Donald Kirkpatrick in 1959, is a well-known and widely used model for evaluating training and development programs (Ulum, 2015). It consists of four levels, which provide a framework to assess the results and impact of such programs from both individual and organizational perspectives. Originally, Kirkpatrick's model had four steps, but it later became recognized as four levels and gained widespread acceptance (Alsalamah & Callinan, 2021; Liao & Hsu, 2019; Dalimunthe 2022). To gain a better understanding of the model, detailed explanations of each of the four levels are provided below.

Level 1: Reaction

At this level, the focus is on measuring participants' immediate reactions and feelings regarding the training program. The assessment involves gathering feedback on their impressions, satisfaction, and engagement with the training (McElfish et al., 2017; Dewi & Kartowagiran, 2018). Common methods include participant surveys and questionnaires, with the primary goal being to gauge participants' perceptions of the training's quality and relevance to their needs. This feedback helps assess how well participants liked the training content, materials, instructors, facilities, and training approaches, as well as whether they found it engaging and relevant to their job roles (Novak et al., 2022). Level 1 is crucial for understanding participant reactions and satisfaction, with the findings providing valuable input for program improvement.

Level 2: Learning

At this level, the focus shifts to assessing the extent to which participants acquired new knowledge, skills, or competencies as a result of the training. Level 2 evaluates learning or knowledge acquisition and is considered a formative evaluation in the context of instructional design and program development. Formative evaluation aims to provide feedback and make necessary adjustments during program development to ensure effectiveness and goal attainment (Yaqoot & Mat, 2021). Evaluation methods may include quizzes, tests, simulations, or observations of participant performance (Hayes et al., 2016). The primary aim is to determine whether participants learned from the training and whether they can apply their new knowledge and skills to their job tasks. This assessment occurs during or immediately after the training program and offers insights for program improvement by identifying areas where participants may not be learning as expected.

Level 3: Behaviors

This level assesses changes in behavior and job performance resulting from the training. It involves observing participants in their work environment to identify changes in their job-related behavior, such as improved performance or the adoption of new skills. The focus is on determining whether the training positively impacted workplace behavior. Level 3 evaluation is more complex and time-consuming than the previous levels. It focuses on assessing changes in participants' behavior and job performance, including the application of newly acquired knowledge and skills in their work roles. This level measures intermediate outcomes and how the training program influenced participants' actions and job-related behavior.

Level 4: Results

Level 4 evaluates the ultimate outcomes and results of the training program in relation to business goals and objectives. Measures may include increased productivity, reduced errors, improved customer satisfaction, increased sales, higher profits, or other key performance indicators relevant to the organization. Level 4 aims to establish a clear connection between the training program and its impact on the organization's bottom line. It goes beyond individual behavior changes to assess the broader impact of the training on the organization, measuring tangible results directly linked to the organization's goals and overall performance.

From the description above, it's evident that each level involves specific evaluation objectives and focus points. These objectives can be further detailed into evaluation questions, which are represented in Table 6.1 for each level.

Kirkpatrick's model is often represented as a pyramid, with each level building upon the one below it. The model is valuable for organizations to assess the effectiveness of their training efforts and make data-driven decisions about how to improve training programs or allocate resources. The levels are arranged in hierarchical order. Therefore, some view the higher levels as more crucial than the lower ones. Many HRD programs are designed to evaluate from Levels 3 and 4. However, Kirkpatrick

Table 6.1 Evaluation objectives and sample questions at each level based on Kirkpatrick's four-level evaluation model

Levels	Evaluation objectives	Sample questions
Level 1: reaction	Participant satisfaction	How satisfied were participants with the training program?
	Engagement	Did participants find the training engaging and relevant to their job roles?
	Quality assessment	What is the perception of the quality of the training content, materials, instructors, and facilities?
	Relevance	Did participants believe the training was relevant to their needs and job responsibilities?
	Improvement suggestions	Can participants provide specific suggestions for improving the training program?
Level 2: learning	Knowledge acquisition	Have participants acquired new knowledge, skills, or competencies through the training?
	Performance change	Can participants demonstrate changes in attitude, knowledge, and skill due to their participation in the training?
	Formative feedback	What evidence supports that participants have gained knowledge and skills?
	Application	Are participants able to apply their newfound knowledge and skills to their job tasks?
	Areas of improvement	Where do participants seem to struggle in their learning, and what adjustments could improve learning outcomes?
Level 3: behaviors	Behavioral changes	Have there been observable changes in participants' job-related behavior as a result of the training?
	Workplace impact	How has the training influenced workplace behavior and performance?
	Application of knowledge	Can participants effectively apply the newly acquired knowledge and skills in their work roles?
	Intermediate outcomes	What intermediate outcomes, such as improved job performance, can be attributed to the training program?
	Challenges	What challenges or barriers hinder participants from consistently applying what they learned on the job?
Level 4: results	Business outcomes	What are the tangible business outcomes resulting from the training, such as increased productivity, reduced errors, improved customer satisfaction, or higher sales?
	Alignment with goals	To what extent has the training program contributed to achieving organizational goals and objectives?
	Impact on profitability	Can the training program be linked to increased profits or cost savings for the organization?
	Key performance indicators	How has the training affected key performance indicators that are relevant to the organization's success?
	Overall impact	What is the broader impact of the training on the organization's bottom line and long-term performance?

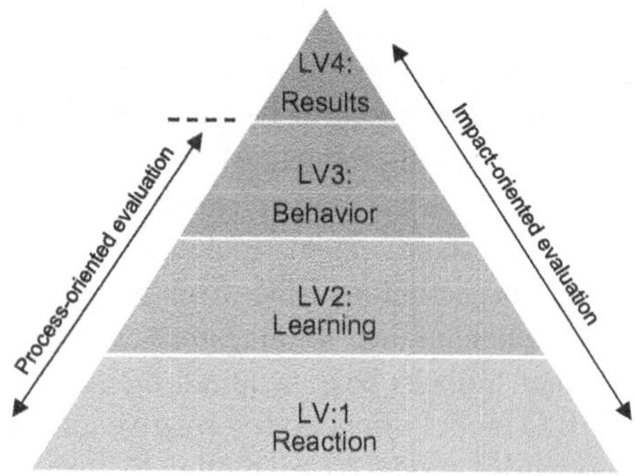

Fig. 6.1 The Kirkpatrick 4-level model pyramid (own illustration, adapted from Kirkpatrick's model)

and Kirkpatrick (2006) contend that the decision to skip the first two levels could easily lead to the wrong conclusion about the effectiveness of the intervention and the training program itself. This is because Level 3 is categorized as outcome evaluation, and Level 4 is categorized as impact evaluation. It's important to note that both levels are interconnected, and Level 4 outcomes often depend on the successful achievement of Level 3 behavior changes. However, the first two levels are also important to provide feedback for program development during the implementation process (Fig. 6.1).

Importantly, all four levels of the Kirkpatrick Model are interconnected, and evaluating only one level may not provide a complete picture of a training program's effectiveness. Levels 1 (Reaction), 2 (Learning), and 3 (Behavior) provide important insights into the process of training, participant engagement, and skill acquisition. Organizations often use a combination of all four levels to get a comprehensive view of the training's impact. Moreover, it's worth noting that Kirkpatrick emphasizes the significance of Level 3 because, without a change in behavior (performance), achieving Level 4 results is not possible (Pineda, 2010; Praslova, 2010; Ross et al., 2022). Despite its challenges, Level 4 is where organizations can genuinely assess the overall impact of their training efforts. While the Kirkpatrick model has remained popular due to its simplicity and practicality, it has also faced criticism over the past decades. This criticism will be thoroughly discussed in a later section.

Kirkpatrick and Bushnell Evaluation Model

Bushnell's IPO (Input, Process, Output) model (Bushnell, 1990) provides a comprehensive evaluation framework that focuses on the entire HR training process. This model encompasses three key stages: input, process, and output. In the input stage, various factors that influence training effectiveness, such as trainer competence, materials, facilities, and equipment, are considered. The process stage involves the planning, design, development, and delivery of the training program. The output stage assesses the short-term benefits, including participants' reactions, knowledge acquisition, and improved job performance, corresponding to Kirkpatrick's first three levels. Importantly, Bushnell extends the model to include Kirkpatrick's fourth level, emphasizing long-term benefits for organizations, such as profitability, customer satisfaction, and productivity.

The IPO Model draws elements from Kirkpatrick's four-level model and Brinkerhoff's six-stage model, making it the preferred choice for corporate training programs, including IBM. This model facilitates organizations in evaluating the achievement of their training goals, identifying areas for improvement, and assessing whether trainees have acquired the necessary knowledge and skills. Furthermore, the IPO model offers both formative and summative information, going beyond the Kirkpatrick model by attempting to quantify the value of training in financial terms. Both Kirkpatrick's Four-Level Model and the Bushnell IPO Model share the common objective of evaluating training programs to determine their effectiveness and impact. However, they differ in their approach and scope of evaluation.

The Bushnell IPO Model stands out as a more comprehensive and systematic framework for assessing training initiatives. It places a strong emphasis on considering every aspect of the HR training process. By incorporating three key stages—input, process, and output—this model evaluates not only the outcomes of training but also the entire journey. It delves into the factors that influence the effectiveness of training programs, such as the competence of trainers, quality of materials, adequacy of facilities, and equipment. This level of detail provides organizations with a holistic view of their training efforts.

Where the Bushnell IPO Model truly shines is in its financially oriented approach. It goes beyond the qualitative assessment typically associated with training evaluation. Instead, it attempts to quantify the value of training in monetary terms. This financial perspective is of particular interest to corporate training programs, as it allows them to demonstrate the real impact of training on an organization's bottom line. The model doesn't stop at short-term benefits like participant reactions, knowledge acquisition, or job performance. It extends the evaluation to long-term organizational benefits, such as increased profitability, heightened customer satisfaction, and improved productivity.

For corporate training programs, which often have a direct influence on an organization's success, this financial aspect is of paramount importance. It enables them to provide concrete evidence of their contributions and justify the investments made in training. By offering a more comprehensive, systematic, and financially focused approach, the Bushnell IPO Model becomes an invaluable tool for corporate training programs seeking to prove their worth and showcase the positive impact they have on the organization's overall success.

While Kirkpatrick's model concentrates on assessing the outcomes and impacts after training, the Bushnell IPO Model offers a more systematic and detailed analysis that encompasses all aspects of the training process. This key distinction makes the Bushnell IPO Model particularly valuable for organizations, especially corporate training programs, seeking a broader and more financially oriented view of their training initiatives (Islam & Hosen, 2021).

Kirkpatrick and Warr et al. Evaluation Model

Warr et al.'s CIRO Model (Cheung et al., 2023) is characterized by its comprehensive and contemporary approach to assessing training programs. What sets it apart is its recognition of the complex interplay between program-specific elements and the broader contextual factors that can influence program effectiveness. In essence, the CIRO Model offers a more nuanced perspective on program evaluation. It acknowledges that training programs do not operate in isolation; they are affected by the environment, culture, and external influences within the organization. This contemporary outlook reflects the evolving nature of HR practices and the need for more holistic and context-aware evaluation methods.

Both Kirkpatrick's Four-Level Model and the CIRO Model play a crucial role in the toolkit of HR professionals and organizations (Dhankhar, 2020). Kirkpatrick's model provides a well-established and time-tested framework that offers a structured approach to program evaluation, focusing on outcomes and impact. On the other hand, the CIRO Model complements this historical perspective by providing a modern and nuanced approach that accounts for the intricate relationship between program-specific factors and the broader organizational context. HR professionals can choose the model that best aligns with their goals, context, and the level of detail they require when assessing the effectiveness of their training programs. Ultimately, having access to both historical and contemporary evaluation frameworks equips HR practitioners with a range of tools to enhance HR practices and achieve organizational goals.

The critical difference is in the flexibility and adaptability of the CIRO Model, as it acknowledges the complex interplay of various elements that influence the effectiveness of training programs. Organizations and HR professionals can choose the model that best suits their specific evaluation needs and the level of detail they require to assess training program effectiveness.

Kirkpatrick and Stufflebeam and Zhang Evaluation Model

Stufflebeam and Zhang's CIPP Model (Stufflebeam & Zhang, 2017) represents a more modern, versatile, and sophisticated approach to evaluating programs. CIPP stands for Context, Input, Process, and Product, offering a comprehensive method that delves deeper into program evaluation. It takes into account contextual factors and their interaction with the program, ensuring a more comprehensive analysis. This model encourages a more nuanced and in-depth understanding of the influences shaping program outcomes and offers a broader view of the entire program life cycle.

One of the standout features of the CIPP Model is its commitment to a holistic evaluation process. It not only scrutinizes the various elements within the program but also explores how the program interacts with its context and the dynamic interplay of these factors. This approach facilitates a more profound understanding of the intricate web of influences that shape the program's outcomes. By looking at the broader program life cycle, this model allows organizations to gain insights into how a program evolves over time, adapts to changes, and ultimately contributes to its intended objectives.

The decision between these models is contingent on an organization's specific evaluation objectives. Kirkpatrick's model is suitable for straightforward and established assessment needs, especially for those organizations that seek a clear and direct understanding of training outcomes (Kirkpatrick, 2006; Ginting et al., 2020). In contrast, the CIPP Model is a more intricate choice, ideal for organizations looking for a more nuanced and comprehensive evaluation process, especially when considering various contextual factors that might influence program effectiveness. The model selection should align with an organization's specific evaluation requirements and the depth of analysis they aim to achieve.

Additional Evaluation Models Resembling Kirkpatrick's Model

There are several other well-established and widely used evaluation models that play a crucial role in the field of Human Resource Development (HRD). As we delve into these additional models, it is essential to bear in mind Kirkpatrick's four-level evaluation framework, which serves as a foundational reference point. It's worth noting that many of these alternative models are, in some way, variations or customizations of Kirkpatrick's original four-level structure, demonstrating the enduring influence and adaptability of his work within the field of HRD (Table 6.2).

Despite a plethora of human resource training evaluation models have been developed as tools to identify the critical dimensions and factors for effective evaluation over the years. Critics, however, have raised concerns about Kirkpatrick's model, primarily centered on its simplicity and lack of consideration for the organizational context. They have also questioned the causal relations between the evaluation levels (Reio Jr. et al., 2017).

Criticisms of Kirkpatrick's Evaluation

The Kirkpatrick Model, despite its widespread use, has faced several critiques and criticisms over the years. The model tends to place more emphasis on Levels 1 (Reaction) and 2 (Learning) while giving relatively less attention to Levels 3 (Behavior) and 4 (Results). The criticism lies in the uneven treatment of these levels. The first two levels, being easier to assess and more immediate in their outcomes, tend to get more focus, while the latter two, which are more complex and require longer observation periods to measure, receive less attention. This imbalance can lead to incomplete evaluations, with a narrower focus on short-term, easily observed metrics

Table 6.2 Comparison of HRD evaluation models

Model by	Description
Brinkerhoff (1988)	Brinkerhoff's six-stage evaluation approach incorporates formative and summative evaluation and integrates the additional stages of goal setting, program design, and immediate, intermediate, and long-term outcomes. However, implementing such a comprehensive evaluation model can be demanding due to various practical constraints
Brinkerhoff (2003)	Brinkerhoff introduced the Success Case Method (SCM) for evaluation, aiming to answer questions about what is happening, the program's impact, its value, and ways to improve it. SCM has the advantage of being able to identify critical success factors on the job, but it requires some judgment in identifying these factors
Dessinger and Moseley (2009)	Dessinger and Moseley's Full-Scope Evaluation Model blends performance improvement and evaluation, combining formative, summative, confirmative, and meta-evaluation. However, it requires long-term organizational support and can be resource-intensive
Holton (1996)	Holton's HRD Evaluation and Research Model postulates three outcome levels: learning, individual performance, and organizational performance. Critics argue that this model does not account for feedback loops and interactions between factors of the same type
Kaufman and Keller's (1994)	Kaufman and Keller proposed an expanded five-level evaluation framework, which extends the scope to internal and external consequences, societal impact, resource availability, and efficiency
Passmore and Velez (2012)	The SOAP-M (Self, Other, Achievements, Potential, Meta-analysis) Model comprises five analysis levels, serving as a framework for HR interventions like training and coaching. It encompasses four levels for HR professionals and an additional fifth level designed for researchers
Phillips (1998)	Phillips' ROI (Return on Investment) framework, emerging in the past decade, has added a fifth level to Kirkpatrick's model to measure success in the HR function, specifically by comparing monetary benefits with program costs. Although it emphasizes return on investment, it faces limitations in determining returns on soft aspects of business, especially in non-controlled environments where isolating intervention effects can be challenging
Swanson (1999)	Swanson's performance improvement evaluation model aims to improve performance through three evaluation levels and assesses performance, learning, and satisfaction. While it resembles Kirkpatrick's model, it emphasizes practical research-based tools and doesn't explicitly cover Kirkpatrick's level three

while overlooking the more challenging, yet impactful, long-term behavioral changes and organizational results that the training should ideally aim to achieve (Reio Jr. et al., 2017).

Arguably, the model can potentially lead organizations to prioritize participant satisfaction and knowledge acquisition over the real-world application and impact of training. This concern revolves around the notion that this emphasis might steer organizations towards valuing surface-level indicators of training success rather than the more profound and substantial changes that can occur. While satisfaction and learning are undoubtedly important, they serve as intermediary goals that ultimately lead to more substantial outcomes, such as changes in behavior and tangible improvements in organizational results. Overemphasizing the initial levels could inadvertently divert attention away from the broader objectives of training, such as its influence on job performance, its ability to induce changes in behaviors, and its impact on organizational success. As a result, there may be limitations in terms of observing and evaluating the practical application of acquired knowledge in the workplace and the overall influence on the organization's performance (Appannah et al., 2017; Ashofteh & Orangian, 2021).

Utilizing the higher levels (Levels 3 and 4) of Kirkpatrick's Model for training evaluation can indeed be challenging. This challenge arises from the depth and complexity inherent in evaluating these higher levels, demanding substantial investments in terms of resources and time to achieve a more comprehensive and accurate evaluation. It requires strategic planning, resource allocation, and a firm commitment from the organization to overcome these challenges and conduct thorough evaluations that delve beyond surface-level assessments of training effectiveness. In reality, however, many organizations tend to prioritize quicker and more immediate feedback on training effectiveness (Dorri et al., 2016). This preference for expediency can pose a significant challenge in practical implementation.

Finally, another crucial aspect to be aware of is that in practical scenarios, different levels might not occur in a sequential order; instead, they could overlap or happen simultaneously. This criticism is crucial as it highlights the discrepancy between the model's theoretical structure and the complex reality of evaluating training programs. It emphasizes the need for a flexible approach to evaluations that considers non-linear progressions, providing a more realistic and adaptable method for analyzing the effectiveness of training programs.

Concluding Remarks

The chapter embarked on a robust journey, conducting an in-depth exploration, critical analysis, and comprehensive comparison of several notable evaluation models. Kirkpatrick, Bushnell, Warr et al., and Stufflebeam and Zhang, along with other renowned models, were thoroughly examined, unraveling the diverse array of frameworks available for the assessment of outcomes and impacts within human resource research.

This detailed examination aimed to shed light on the multifaceted nature of evaluating human resource training and development. Each model, with its unique structure, offers different lenses through which to evaluate training effectiveness. The comparison and critique showcased the varied strengths and limitations of each, guiding practitioners toward a nuanced understanding of how each model operates within distinct organizational contexts.

The comprehensive comparison sought to offer clarity and direction, empowering HR professionals and researchers to make informed decisions about which evaluation models best align with their organizational needs and strategic objectives. By providing such detailed insights, this chapter aspires to equip practitioners with the knowledge to select, adapt, or combine evaluation models effectively, tailoring their approach to suit specific organizational requirements and training programs.

Through this exploration, the chapter aimed to contribute to the ongoing evolution of the field of human resource research. By fostering an in-depth understanding of these evaluation methodologies, it helps organizations refine their approaches, leading to evidence-based practices that enable the alignment of training programs with strategic goals. It is within this context that the chapter seeks to facilitate a more profound comprehension of training program effectiveness and their influences on organizational performance and success.

References

Alsalamah, A., & Callinan, C. (2021). Adaptation of Kirkpatrick's four-level model of training criteria to evaluate training programmes for head teachers. *Education Sciences, 11*(3), 116–130.

Appannah, A., Meyer, C., Ogrin, R., McMillan, S., Barrett, E., & Browning, C. (2017). Diversity training for the community aged care workers: A conceptual framework for evaluation. *Evaluation and Program Planning, 63*, 74–81.

Ashofteh, H., & Orangian, E. (2021). Evaluating the effectiveness and calculating the rate of return on investment of training courses using Kirk Patrick and Phillips models. *Management and Educational Perspective, 3*(3), 143–179.

Bari, S., Incorvia, J., Iverson, K. R., Bekele, A., Garringer, K., Ahearn, O., Drown, L., Emiru, A. A., Burssa, D., Workineh, S., Sheferaw, E. D., Meara, J. G., & Beyene, A. (2021). Surgical data strengthening in Ethiopia: Results of a Kirkpatrick framework evaluation of a data quality intervention. *Global Health Action, 14*(1), 1855808.

Brinkerhoff, R. O. (1988). An integrated evaluation model for HRD. *Training & Development Journal, 42*(2), 66–69.

Brinkerhoff, R. (2003). *The success case method: Find out quickly what's working and what's not.* Berrett-Koehler Publishers.

Bushnell, D. S. (1990). Input, process, output: A model for evaluating training. *Training and Development Journal, 44*(3), 41–43.

Cheung, V. K. L., Chia, N. H., So, S. S., Ng, G. W. Y., & So, E. H. K. (2023). Expanding scope of Kirkpatrick model from training effectiveness review to evidence-informed prioritization management for cricothyroidotomy simulation. *Heliyon, 9*(8), 1–15.

Dalimunthe, M. B. (2022). Kirkpatrick four-level model evaluation: An evaluation scale on the preservice teacher's internship program. *Journal of Education Research and Evaluation, 6*(2), 367–376.

Dessinger, J. C., & Moseley, J. L. (2009). Full-scope evaluation: Do you "really oughta, wanna"? In *Handbook of improving performance in the workplace: Volumes 1–3* (pp. 128–141).

Dewi, L. R., & Kartowagiran, B. (2018). An evaluation of internship program by using Kirkpatrick evaluation model. *REID (Research and Evaluation in Education), 4*(2), 155–163.

Dhankhar, K. (2020). Training effectiveness evaluation models. A comparison. *Indian Journal of Training and Development, 3*, 66–73.

Dorri, S., Akbari, M., & Sedeh, M. D. (2016). Kirkpatrick evaluation model for in-service training on cardiopulmonary resuscitation. *Iranian Journal of Nursing and Midwifery Research, 21*(5), 493.

Ginting, H., Mahiranissa, A., Bekti, R., & Febriansyah, H. (2020). The effect of outing team building training on soft skills among MBA students. *The International Journal of Management Education, 18*(3), 100423.

Hayes, H., Scott, V., Abraczinskas, M., Scaccia, J., Stout, S., & Wandersman, A. (2016). A formative multi-method approach to evaluating training. *Evaluation and Program Planning, 58*, 199–207.

Holton, E. F., III. (1996). The flawed four-level evaluation model. *Human Resource Development Quarterly, 7*(1), 5–21.

Islam, M. Z., & Hosen, S. (2021). An effectiveness study on policy level training course: A case from Bangladesh Public Administration Training Centre, Bangladesh. *Asian Journal of Education and Social Studies, 18*(3), 41–52.

Kaufman, R., & Keller, J. M. (1994). Levels of evaluation: Beyond Kirkpatrick. *Human resource development quarterly, 5*(4), 371–380.

Kirkpatrick, D., & Kirkpatrick, J. (2006). *Evaluating training programs: The four levels*. Berrett-Koehler Publishers.

Kirkpatrick, D. L. (2006). Seven keys to unlock the four levels of evaluation. *Performance Improvement, 45*(7), 5–8.

Liao, S. C., & Hsu, S. Y. (2019). Evaluating a continuing medical education program: New world Kirkpatrick model approach. *International Journal of Management, Economics and Social Sciences (IJMESS), 8*(4), 266–279.

Lim, D. H., Yoon, S. W., & Park, S. (2013). Integrating learning outcome typologies for HRD: Review and current status. *New Horizons in Adult Education and Human Resource Development, 25*(2), 33–48.

Malik, S., & Asghar, M. Z. (2020). In-service early childhood education teachers' training program evaluation through Kirkpatrick model. *Journal of Research, 14*(2), 259–270.

McElfish, P. A., Long, C. R., Rowland, B., Moore, S., Wilmoth, R., & Ayers, B. (2017). Improving culturally appropriate care using a community-based participatory research approach: Evaluation of a multicomponent cultural competency training program, Arkansas, 2015–2016. *Preventing Chronic Disease, 14*, E62.1–11.

Novak, D. A., Hawks, B. A., Revere, F. L., & Hallowell, R. (2022). *Sustainability in a health systems science program: Assessment, evaluation, and continuous improvement. Health systems science education: Development and implementation*. E-Book: Vol. 4 in the AMA MedEd Innovation Series, 4 (p. 103).

Passmore, J., & Velez, M. (2012). SOAP-M: A training evaluation model for HR. *Industrial and Commercial Training, 44*(6), 315–325.

Phillips, J. J. (1998). The return-on-investment (ROI) process: Issues and trends. *Educational Technology, 38*(4), 7–14.

Pineda, P. (2010). Evaluation of training in organisations: A proposal for an integrated model. *Journal of European Industrial Training, 34*(7), 673–693.

Praslova, L. (2010). Adaptation of Kirkpatrick's four level model of training criteria to assessment of learning outcomes and program evaluation in higher education. *Educational Assessment, Evaluation and Accountability, 22*, 215–225.

Reio, T. G., Jr., Rocco, T. S., Smith, D. H., & Chang, E. (2017). A critique of Kirkpatrick's evaluation model. *New Horizons in Adult Education and Human Resource Development, 29*(2), 35–53.

Ross, B., Penkunas, M. J., Maher, D., Certain, E., & Launois, P. (2022). Evaluating results of the implementation research MOOC using Kirkpatrick's four-level model: A cross-sectional mixed-methods study. *British Medical Journal Open, 12*(5), e054719.

Sinclair, P., Kable, A., & Levett-Jones, T. (2015). The effectiveness of internet-based e-learning on clinician behavior and patient outcomes: A systematic review protocol. *JBI Evidence Synthesis, 13*(1), 52–64.

Strekalova, Y. A. L., Qin, Y. S., Sharma, S., Nicholas, J., McCaslin, G. P., Forman, K. E., et al. (2021). The black voices in research curriculum to promote diversity and inclusive excellence in biomedical research. *Journal of Clinical and Translational Science, 5*(1), e206.

Stufflebeam, D. L., & Zhang, G. (2017). *The CIPP evaluation model: How to evaluate for improvement and accountability*. Guilford Publications.

Swanson, R. A. (1999). The foundations of performance improvement and implications for practice. *Advances in Developing Human Resources, 1*(1), 1–25.

Ulum, Ö. G. (2015). Program evaluation through Kirkpatrick's framework. *Online Submission, 8*(1), 106–111.

von Thiele Schwarz, U., Lundmark, R., & Hasson, H. (2016). The dynamic integrated evaluation model (DIEM): Achieving sustainability in organizational intervention through a participatory evaluation approach. *Stress and Health, 32*(4), 285–293.

Warr, P. B., Bird, M. W., & Rackham, N. (1970). *Evaluation of management training: A practical framework, with cases, for evaluating training needs and results*. Gower Press.

Williams, R. C., & Nafukho, F. M. (2015). Technical training evaluation revisited: An exploratory, mixed-methods study. *Performance Improvement Quarterly, 28*(1), 69–93.

Yaqoot, E. S. I., & Mat, N. (2021). Determination of training material and organisational culture impact in vocational training effectiveness in Bahrain. *Journal of Technical Education and Training, 13*(4), 1–14.

Chapter 7
Determining Outcomes and Impacts of Human Resource Research with Participatory Evaluation

Introduction

The pursuit of evaluating the outcomes and impacts of research initiatives remains a persistent challenge. As organizations endeavor to optimize their human resources and adapt to the evolving demands of the contemporary global workforce, the role of research in Human Resource Development (HRD) has gained paramount significance (Sambhalwal & Kaur, 2023). Yet, the mere execution of research in this field falls short; equally crucial is the systematic assessment of its outcomes and the far-reaching impacts it engenders.

Participatory evaluation involves a collaborative approach that assembles diverse stakeholders, including researchers, practitioners, employees, and organizational leaders, to engage in a collective evaluation of the research process and its subsequent outcomes (Bosma et al., 2022). Through this collaborative endeavor, a more nuanced and enriched understanding of the research's impact emerges, encompassing not only the evident results but also the underlying, often subtle, and latent influences that extend across various dimensions of human resources within organizations (Ferguson et al, 2017).

Beyond theoretical exploration, this chapter aims to bridge the gap between scholarly discourse and practical application. Through the analysis of participatory evaluation methodologies and their integration into the determination of HR research outcomes and impacts, it strives to offer practical insights and actionable recommendations that can enhance the effectiveness and value of HRD initiatives (Ketola et al., 2007). Consequently, the ensuing sections of this chapter will delve into the theoretical foundations, methodological approaches, practical implications, and potential consequences of embracing participatory evaluation as an intrinsic component of the HRD research process. This exploration seeks to contribute to the evolving discourse surrounding the application of participatory evaluation in the context of HRD, thus enriching the scholarly conversation and the real-world impact of this transformative approach.

N. Kiettikunwong and P. Narot, *Determining Outcomes and Impacts of Human Resource Development Programs*, https://doi.org/10.1007/978-981-97-0395-1_7

Rise of Participatory Evaluation

The evaluation serves a specific purpose: to obtain information that enhances capacity building and effective management within organizations. Human Resource Development (HRD), the process of helping employees grow and improve their skills, knowledge, and abilities to contribute more effectively to their organization's success, is crucial for enhancing individuals within organizations. This process includes training, development, and other activities that support employee growth and the overall goals of the organization (Doufexi & Pampouri, 2022). These are key factors in individual performance development and the success of organizations in achieving expected outcomes, as organizations depend on individuals' capacity to perform tasks. Therefore, the design of the evaluation approach is crucial for obtaining information to enhance the development of human resource development programs, which can potentially impact the increase or decrease in their employees' potential. However, interesting issues persist regarding which evaluation approaches would be appropriate for assessing potential and effectively extracting the information needed to improve the HRD process or support employees.

While the positivist foundation—a philosophical approach that relies on empirical observation, scientific methods, and objective measurements to understand the world, emphasizes concrete, measurable data in research and analysis—has strongly influenced traditional evaluation approaches, its limitations are evident. This is because positivism tends to emphasize the significance of empirical observation, scientific methodology, and the objective measurement of phenomena. Consequently, it may not fully capture the complexity and wide spectrum of HRD programs (Erciyes, 2020; Williams, 2020). For instance, consider a scenario in which a traditional positivist evaluation approach is applied to measure the effectiveness of a company's HRD program. While this approach might efficiently measure quantifiable factors like the number of training hours completed or test scores of participants, it may overlook the subtler aspects of the program's impact, such as improved teamwork, employee motivation, or leadership development. These qualitative and nuanced aspects, essential for holistic program evaluation, may not be adequately captured by the positivist method, highlighting its limitations in assessing the complexity and wide-ranging impacts of HRD programs.

Furthermore, it has been analyzed that traditional evaluation approaches are often characterized by top-down implementation. They are typically initiated by organizations or driven by executives with centralized decision-making processes. These methods frequently involve minimal input from the individuals and groups directly affected by the evaluation. This lack of input can hinder the organization's ability to thrive as it may lead to a deficiency in understanding their needs and priorities. Moreover, the rigidity and inflexibility of these approaches make it challenging to adapt to changing circumstances or evolving project requirements. Consequently, stakeholders may have reduced ownership and engagement in the process, potentially leading to resistance or a lack of commitment.

An example of a traditional top-down evaluation approach falling short is evident in educational institutions' assessment systems. In many schools, assessments and evaluation processes are often designed and imposed by educational boards or administrative bodies without extensive input from teachers, students, or parents. These standardized evaluation systems typically emphasize 'high-stakes' testing to measure student performance. However, these tests may not comprehensively address the diverse learning needs or the full spectrum of a student's abilities. Students have unique learning styles, strengths, and weaknesses that standardized tests may not adequately capture. Consequently, the evaluation system may not fully represent the quality of education or the individual progress of each student (Bin Othayman et al., 2022). This system often neglects the involvement of teachers, who work closely with students and understand their individual needs. Despite their valuable insights and suggestions, which could be incredibly helpful, they may not be adequately integrated into the evaluation methods. Thus, this type of traditional top-down evaluation approach undeniably limits the assessment's ability to effectively measure and enhance the overall educational experience (Song, 2004).

Conversely, participatory evaluation is a bottom-up approach. It is participant-driven, with participants serving as joint evaluators alongside professional evaluators. It involves open decision-making, shared ownership of the program with involved parties, and is based on a flexible and responsive evaluation plan designed and implemented in collaboration with participants (Cousins & Earl, 1992; Choi & Park, 2022). This may be why Participatory Evaluation has been widely implemented in national and international development programs since the late 1970s (Cullen & Coryn, 2011).

In addition, Participatory Evaluation is introduced as an extension of the stakeholder-based model, with a specific emphasis on enhancing the utilization of evaluations. This is accomplished by actively involving a diverse group of participants in the research or development program process. It's worth noting that Participatory Action Research—a collaborative research approach that involves both researchers and the community, working together to create positive change—is also a component of this evaluative process. Furthermore, for the benefit of the academic community seeking a comprehensive understanding of this concept, Cousins and Earl (1992) have offered valuable insights, which are summarized in Table 7.1.

Lastly, O'Sullivan and D'Agostino (2002), Weaver and Cousin (2004) explained that the term 'participatory evaluation' is used interchangeably with 'participation' and 'empowerment evaluation.' Some literature also categorizes participatory evaluation as collaboration evaluation (Ryan et al., 1998). Despite variations in how participatory evaluation is operationalized, in practice, participatory evaluation is known as an approach for assessing and evaluating programs, projects, policies, or initiatives that actively involve the people affected by or involved in the program in the evaluation process (Cullen et al., 2011). It is a collaborative and inclusive approach that seeks to empower stakeholders and promote their active participation in designing, conducting, and interpreting evaluations. The individuals involved, including program participants, community members, staff, funders, and other relevant parties (stakeholders), take part in various stages of the evaluation process. This

Table 7.1 Functions of participatory evaluation and stakeholder-based evaluation

Participatory evaluation	Stakeholder-based evaluation
Involves a relatively small number of primary users	Involves a large number of potential organization members to build support
Engages the primary users in essential functions, including problem formulation, instrument design, data collection, analysis, interpretation, recommendation, and reporting	Engages organization members in a consultative manner to clarify the context and establish evaluation questions. This involvement may include connections to research and practice-based communities, facilitating communication links, establishing direct contacts between personnel from both communities, and fostering collaborative participation in the project
The evaluator serves as the project coordinator and is responsible for technical support, training, quality control, and joint program management	The evaluator serves as the principal investigator, responsible for translating institutional requirements into a program
Personnel training activities, critical for the program, are supervised and conducted by the evaluator to facilitate on-the-job learning	Places less emphasis on enhancing utilization in the context of organizational learning

approach allows for the selection of evaluation methods and tools that are most appropriate for the specific context and stakeholders involved, while its flexibility can lead to more accurate and meaningful results (Gasparatos & Scolobig, 2012). Besides, in certain practices, the approach is employed with the goals of: (1) increasing the use of evaluation findings, (2) including a wide range of stakeholders in identifying evaluation questions, and (3) involving them in the evaluation process (Weiss, 1983). Ultimately, this means that the Participatory Evaluation approach does not allow the evaluator to fully control the decision-making process alone (non top-down) and has remained one of the popular choices to this day (Cullen & Coryn, 2011; Pollock et al., 2019).

Methodological Approaches of Participatory Evaluation

In the context of participatory evaluation, the process of assessing programs and projects is unique. Unlike traditional evaluation methods, participatory evaluation actively involves a wide range of people connected to the program being assessed. These individuals may include program participants, community members, staff, funders, or policymakers. The involvement of such a diverse group of stakeholders adds complexity to the evaluation process because each group has distinct priorities. For instance, program participants are primarily concerned with how the program benefits them, while funders seek to understand the value of their investment, and policymakers consider how the program aligns with their broader plans.

The primary objective of participatory evaluation goes beyond merely measuring the outcomes and impacts of programs. It also aims to comprehend the various factors contributing to these outcomes. Consequently, no single evaluation method can fully capture the entirety of the program's impact, effectiveness, or implications. Using a variety of methods allows evaluators to collect a more comprehensive and well-rounded set of data. This approach facilitates the acquisition of a holistic view of the program's performance and outcomes.

Participatory Evaluation is founded on a fundamental principle that emphasizes a stakeholder approach to assessing training programs. This approach is guided by several key principles. The first principle emphasizes the importance of recognizing the existence of multiple stakeholder groups within an organization (Sambhalwal & Kaur, 2023). These groups could be different departments, teams, or categories of employees, each having a distinct interest in the training programs. The second principle highlights the need to actively involve these stakeholders in the training process. This involvement goes beyond passive participation and includes seeking their input, considering their unique needs and preferences, and ensuring that the training is designed and delivered in a way that aligns with what various stakeholder groups require.

In order for all stakeholders to participate in setting the appropriate direction and goals, engaging in various activities is necessary. These activities are designed to ensure that all stakeholders are actively involved in defining the right direction and objectives. A diverse set of activities is essential for creating an inclusive and collaborative environment where the voices and perspectives of all relevant parties are heard and considered. The overview of the key stages of stakeholder involvement in Participatory Evaluation can be seen in Fig. 7.1.

From the information above, the initial step, known as Needs Assessment, involves identifying all relevant stakeholders in the HRD process. This group comprises employees, managers, HR professionals, trainers, executives, unions, and external partners. These stakeholders collaborate in the identification of HRD needs within the organization. Input is collected from employees, managers, and other pertinent parties to determine the existing skill and knowledge gaps that require attention. This stage serves the crucial purpose of establishing the skills, knowledge, and competencies necessary to achieve organizational goals. It essentially indicates the current state and the need for change. In other words, it prompts organizations, project teams, or individuals to recognize the necessity for change and transition from their current state to reach desired competencies or organizational objectives (Galli, 2018). Needs assessment plays a pivotal role in HRD by aiding organizations in pinpointing gaps in employee knowledge, skills, and abilities (Bin Othayman et al., 2022). This, in turn, enables the development of targeted and effective strategies for training and development efforts (AlYahya et al., 2013).

Secondly, in the Program Design stage, stakeholders collaborate on the development of HRD programs and initiatives. This collaboration involves employees and managers working together on organization and career development plans. Since HRD is an ongoing learning process, the organization's policies and procedures need to incorporate and continually support learning through evaluation. During this

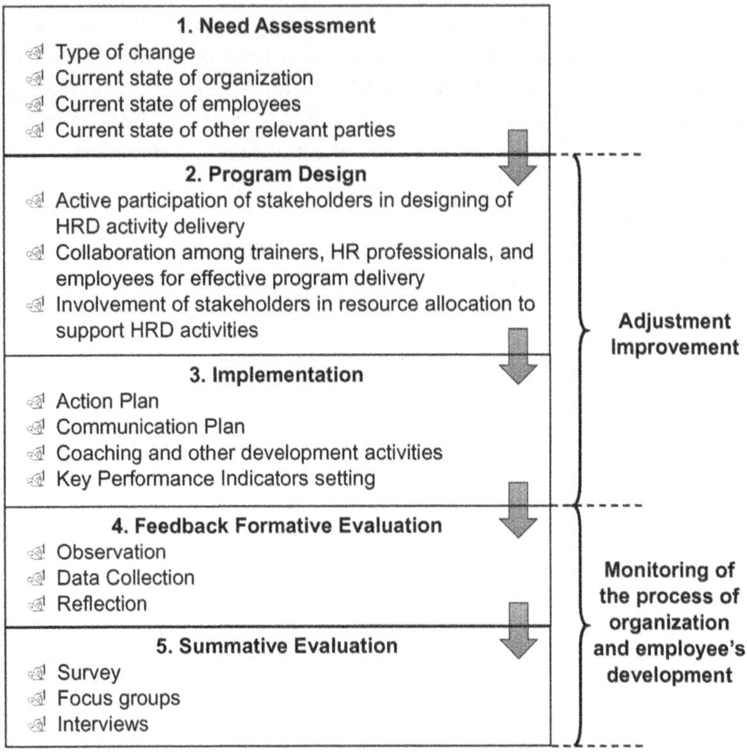

Fig. 7.1 Key stages of stakeholder involvement, activities, and methodologies used in Participatory Evaluation

stage, employees and their supervisors engage in discussions about career goals, potential advancement opportunities, and the necessary skill development.

When stakeholders actively participate in the design and planning of HRD programs, they play a vital role in defining the objectives, content, delivery methods, and evaluation criteria for HRD initiatives. This process lays out the framework for how to conduct specific tasks and activities, facilitating the transition to change, where both individual members and the organization can effectively perform new roles and functions. Importantly, this process should ensure that the overall change aligns with the needs of the stakeholders. In essence, stakeholders contribute their insights regarding the content, format, and delivery methods of training and development programs (Sthapit, 2021).

Thirdly, in the Implementation stage, stakeholders actively participate in the actual delivery of HRD activities. This involvement includes stakeholders like trainers and HR professionals who oversee the execution of HRD programs. They collaborate in delivering training, coaching, and various development activities. This collaborative effort involves trainers, facilitators, and HR professionals working closely with employees and managers to ensure the effective delivery of HRD initiatives.

Additionally, stakeholders may be engaged in resource allocation, including budgets, time, and personnel, to support HRD activities. This allocation process ensures that HRD initiatives receive adequate funding and support.

Fourthly, in the Feedback and Formative Evaluation stage, stakeholders, which include employees and managers, provide feedback on the HRD programs. In particular, participants and their supervisors are instrumental in offering feedback on the effectiveness of HRD programs through a formative evaluation process. This process involves collecting data to assess the ongoing program implementation and reflect on the impact of HRD initiatives. Based on the feedback from stakeholders and the results of the evaluation, HRD programs may be adjusted and improved. Stakeholders are in a position to recommend changes aimed at enhancing program outcomes.

Finally, in the Conducting Summative Evaluation stage, various approaches, such as surveys, focus groups, or interviews, may be employed to gather input on program effectiveness. During this stage, stakeholders remain engaged in monitoring the progress of employees' development. Managers and HR professionals actively track the application of newly acquired skills and knowledge on the job. HR professionals and managers play a crucial role in ensuring that the development efforts result in improved performance.

In summary, in the context of using Participatory Evaluation, the journey through the stages of stakeholder involvement in HRD is a dynamic and essential process. Needs Assessment sets the foundation by involving a diverse array of stakeholders to pinpoint knowledge and skill gaps, paving the way for informed development strategies. Program Design underscores the collaborative role of stakeholders in shaping HRD programs, aligning them with organizational objectives. Implementation sees stakeholders actively engaged in program delivery, and their role extends to resource allocation, ensuring programs receive necessary support. In the Feedback and Formative Evaluation stage, stakeholders provide valuable insights for program enhancement, while Summative Evaluation employs diverse methods to gauge program effectiveness. Throughout this process, stakeholders contribute to the continuous improvement and success of HRD initiatives, demonstrating the significance of their active involvement in HRD's evolution.

The last point pertains to methodological approaches in Participatory Evaluation. HRD programs are interventions for organizational development, and as such, von Thiele Schwarz et al. (2021) emphasizes the need for input from different stakeholders at various stages and for different purposes. Consequently, the implementation and evaluation of HRD require the involvement of employees and management personnel at all levels of the organization to ensure support and ownership throughout the intervention process (Hasson et al., 2014; Kibukho, 2021).

Therefore, von Thiele Schwarz et al. (2021) introduces pragmatic principles for the development of interventions in organizational development:

(1) Ensure active engagement and participation among key stakeholders.
(2) Understand the starting point and objectives of the intervention.
(3) Align the intervention with existing organizational objectives.
(4) Clarify the program's logic.

(5) Prioritize intervention activities based on the effort-gain balance.
(6) Work with existing practices, processes, and mindsets.
(7) Interactively observe, reflect, and react.

This interactive approach to organizational development often aligns with action research, which is a social process of collaborative learning that involves participants and stakeholders in changing practices, interacting, and sharing experiences (Kemmis & McTaggart, 2003). This approach emphasizes group decision-making and a commitment to improving organizational performance (McTaggart, 1991).

In essence, Participatory Action Research can serve as a valuable tool to gain insight into the needs of all stakeholders and facilitate the successful implementation of Participatory Evaluation along with Stakeholder approaches.

An example of Participatory Evaluation in HRD can be found in Chukwu (2015), who studied the case of a Nigerian hospital aiming to enhance training effectiveness for all stakeholders. Participatory Evaluation was employed through action research as an intervention to improve training effectiveness. The process involved using action research to construct, plan, act, and evaluate. The functions of action research included diagnosing and reflecting on the intervention. Data on Participatory Evaluation were generated through focus groups and one-on-one interviews, and template analysis was conducted on reflections related to the intervention.

The study revealed that by identifying and discussing their stakes, contributions, and encouragement in training, participants were able to reflect on their own learning, gain insights into their work situations, and share experiences with the group. This facilitated peer and management support and led to changes in behavior and perceptions. The input from stakeholders was used to improve training design, delivery, and participation. Moreover, participants learned self-directed and self-management skills by being able to discuss workplace problems or issues.

In the subsequent sections, the chapter will delve into the practical implications and potential consequences of integrating participatory evaluation as an integral element of the HRD research process. This exploration will shed light on the real-world applications and impact of implementing participatory evaluation methodologies, highlighting the transformative potential and its effects on HRD initiatives and organizational practices.

Practical Implications of Participatory Evaluation

In the real-world context, employing Participatory Evaluation brings about practical benefits and challenges. These implications encompass the influence of this approach on program design, stakeholder engagement, decision-making, resource allocation, and the overall effectiveness of HRD initiatives in a tangible manner (Kibukho, 2021). These practical considerations and outcomes associated with the adoption of participatory evaluation should be taken into account when contemplating the utilization or design stage of Participatory Evaluation.

In a corporate setting, involving stakeholders in the performance appraisal process can have a transformative impact. Consider a scenario where employees, managers, and HR professionals actively participate in performance evaluations. They feel empowered by the process, sensing that their voices and perspectives matter. This collaborative approach extends beyond mere appraisal; it fosters a sense of ownership in program development. In this environment, HRD activities are seen as vital in nurturing a talent pipeline for future leadership positions. Employees not only receive feedback on their performance but also actively engage in shaping their own career development, aligning their goals with the organization's needs (Barnett & Davis, 2008; Waite, 2013).

The involvement of employees, managers, and HR professionals becomes crucial, especially during organizational change efforts, where stakeholders play a pivotal role in assisting employees in adapting to new roles, technologies, and processes. Throughout these stages, the participation of personnel from different work units and skill sets is essential. Additionally, effective communication, collaboration, and feedback mechanisms are vital for ensuring the success of the organization as it aligns with its objectives, caters to employee needs, and advances broader business strategies through HRD initiatives (Guinan et al., 2019; Mlambo et al., 2021; Stahl et al., 2020). This stresses the notion that the Participatory Evaluation approach is a continuous and evolving process, cultivated within the organization's culture of ongoing learning and development (Slotte et al., 2004).

Imagine the case of a company undergoing a digital transformation,[1] which provides an excellent case study to illustrate the significance of involving employees, managers, and HR professionals during organizational change efforts (Singh et al., 2020). This is particularly evident in the context of transitioning to cloud computing services. This transformation necessitated a shift in skills and processes, and stakeholders played a crucial role in helping employees adapt to these new roles and technologies (Butterfoss et al., 2001; Bennett & McWhorter, 2021).

The first stage involved understanding the current situation, which required the active involvement of stakeholders from various departments within the organization. Once the need for change was identified, stakeholders, including HR professionals, managers, and technical experts, collaborated to design HRD programs aimed at upskilling employees. These programs included training on cloud technologies, data analytics, and cybersecurity, among others. The transition stage was marked by a shift in roles and responsibilities. Personnel from different work units and skill sets were actively involved in learning and development programs (Marion & Fixson, 2021). Employees who were traditionally focused on on-premises solutions had to adapt to the cloud environment, which required new skills and competencies.

Throughout these stages, effective communication and collaboration were pivotal. HR professionals worked closely with managers and technical experts to ensure the successful delivery of training programs. Feedback mechanisms were in place to

[1] Digital transformation is the process of using digital technologies to fundamentally change how a business operates and delivers value to customers.

continuously assess the effectiveness of these HRD initiatives. IBM's HRD transformation was not a one-time event but a continuous and evolving process. The company fostered a culture of ongoing learning and development, where employees were encouraged to continuously update their skills and knowledge to keep up with the ever-changing technology landscape. Not only that IBM's case illustrates how stakeholders, including employees, managers, and HR professionals, played an essential role in navigating a significant organizational change, simultaneously, this case aligns with the principles of Participatory Evaluation as it emphasizes the importance of involving stakeholders in HRD during times of change (Meena et al., 2023).

One crucial issue to keep in mind when conducting Participatory Evaluation is the paramount importance of ethical considerations. Throughout the process, ethics should be at the forefront, ensuring that the rights, dignity, and well-being of all stakeholders are not only acknowledged but also actively protected. This ethical dimension of Participatory Evaluation aligns with broader principles of respect and accountability (Fukuda-Parr & Gibbons, 2021; Hailu, 2013).

It can be concluded that satisfaction and involvement in HRD fosters alignment between HRD efforts and organizational objectives, enhances employee engagement and satisfaction, and promotes a culture of learning and development within the organization. Effective communication and collaboration are essential to ensure the success of HRD initiatives.

It can be firmly concluded that active involvement of stakeholders plays a pivotal role in achieving several highly beneficial outcomes (Chouinard, 2013; Chukwu, 2018). Notably, they foster a robust alignment between HRD efforts and the overarching objectives of the organization. This alignment ensures that HRD activities are intrinsically linked to the strategic goals and vision of the organization, making them more purposeful and impactful (Roxas et al., 2020; Shahzad et al., 2020).

Potential Consequences of Integrating Participatory Evaluation

When Participatory Evaluation becomes an integral part of the process, the consequences of enhanced stakeholder engagement, influencing decision-making, and driving innovation will be diverse and impactful (Stahl et al., 2020). These consequences stem from several factors.

In traditional evaluation approaches, decision-making is typically top-down, resulting in reduced engagement and ownership among those directly affected (Butt, 2021). Conversely, in Participatory Evaluation, the active involvement of stakeholders ensures their insights and concerns are heard and addressed (Nielsen, 2013, 2017). One common hindrance in traditional evaluations is decision-makers lacking a comprehensive understanding of the specific challenges and needs of diverse stakeholder groups due to the absence of accurate and relevant data. Such traditional approaches often prioritize high-level metrics and objectives, potentially missing

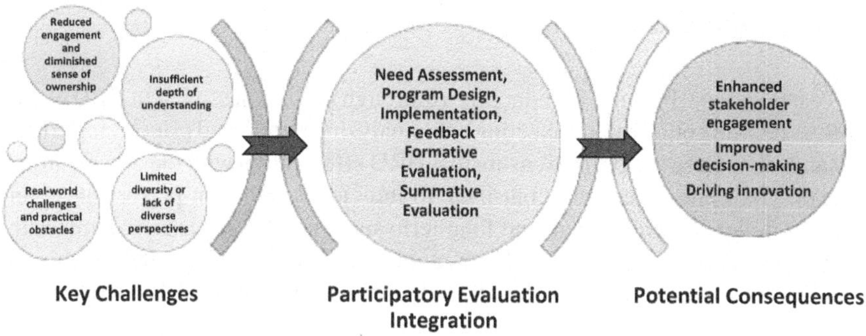

Fig. 7.2 Potential consequences of integrating Participatory Evaluation to address key challenges

critical subtleties in assessing program effectiveness. Additionally, traditional evaluations often rely on standardized methods and predetermined success criteria, sometimes dismissing diverse stakeholder perspectives and innovative ideas. This rigidity can impede the fostering of new solutions or approaches, hindering innovation (Fig. 7.2).

Moreover, Participatory Evaluation is a learning process rooted in the idea that knowledge and values are socially constructed, not existing independently from the social context. Consequently, stakeholders should actively participate in constructing knowledge and skills through the evaluation process, using this knowledge within the organization (von Thiele Schwarz et al., 2021). When stakeholders, especially employees, fully engage in the evaluation process, unique potential consequences, as suggested by AlYahya et al. (2013), can emerge.

Individual Level

When integrating Participatory Evaluation, individuals are more likely to be motivated as they actively participate in the evaluation process. This active involvement leads to a sense of ownership and assurance concerning the training goals and outcomes. Their participation in shaping the evaluation process not only boosts their motivation to engage in HRD activities but also promotes learning at the individual level. Additionally, this aligns individuals with the understanding that knowledge and values are socially constructed and transmitted through social context, closely intertwined with organizational goals (Joseph-Richard & McCray, 2023).

Organizational Level

The organizational benefit of conducting a thorough needs assessment in HRD, which involves defining objectives, collecting data, analyzing trends, and prioritizing critical skill and competency gaps, is to ensure that HRD efforts align with the organization's strategic goals and objectives, contribute to individual and team performance, and support employee development and long-term success. This process maximizes the impact of HRD initiatives by involving input from various stakeholders within the organization and considering factors like alignment with broader HRD strategy and vision.

Societal Level

The integration of participatory practices, such as motivation, conceptual evaluation, and needs assessment, leads to a more motivated and skilled workforce, not only enhancing employee engagement and job satisfaction but also benefiting society at large. By improving training motivation and fostering a culture of learning and development, these practices contribute to the overall societal well-being and advancement by ensuring a workforce that is more skilled, adaptable, and equipped to address the evolving challenges and opportunities in the global job market (Aithal, & Aithal, 2023). This, in turn, promotes economic growth, social progress, and the development of a skilled and competitive workforce that can contribute to society's overall welfare.

Limitation of the Approach

Imagine an integrated Participatory Evaluation approach within an organization aimed at revamping the performance appraisal system. This approach involves several key stages of stakeholder involvement, various activities, and specific methodologies. Repeated meetings with employees and stakeholders are conducted to gather their input on the design of the new system, criteria for evaluation, and data collection methods. Stakeholders are strongly encouraged to participate in this process, providing feedback and suggestions for what they consider a fair and effective performance appraisal system (Esper et al., 2023). The potential positive consequences of this approach could be significant. However, a question arises: why do some, if not the majority, tend to avoid the use of this excellent and inclusive evaluation approach?

Firstly, as mentioned earlier, participatory evaluations genuinely aim to capture voices from all sectors. However, it's essential to acknowledge that not every organization or individual enjoys frequent meetings, and it's important to bear in mind that each meeting comes with associated costs. The numerous meetings and discussions make the process highly time-consuming. This means that organizations must consider opportunity costs when opting for Participatory Evaluation. This constraint can be argued to be a key reason why organizations with limited financial resources, operating in highly competitive and volatile markets that demand swift decision-making, cannot afford the luxury of choosing this type of evaluation model. They must continuously strive to control costs while maintaining their competitiveness in the market to remain highly competitive at all times. Sometimes, organizations may find that opting to replace workers is less expensive than choosing to implement this form of evaluation, resulting in a relatively high turnover in terms of employment. Another point to consider is that there is associated frustration among some stakeholders, such as managers who were eager to see improvements. This frustration arises due to the extended time spent on the lengthy information gathering process, while delayed employee input may complicate the implementation of the new system and lead to issues.

Secondly, in the example provided above, it is evident that while listening to every voice can result in a range of opinions, it is essential to recognize that people within an organization come from diverse backgrounds, each with their own societal values, cultural influences, beliefs, and opinions. As a result, not all opinions will align with each other. This implies that gathering diverse opinions can sometimes be counterproductive to the entire process. When the opinions expressed contain significant conflicts, these conflicts can often escalate into major disputes that cannot be resolved through the evaluation process. Typically, this leads to additional administrative challenges. Moreover, the diverse opinions collected mainly comprise qualitative data, which holds significant value in improving the human resources development process. However, interpreting qualitative data poses challenges, as its analysis depends not only on acquiring data but also on the data interpretation process. Misinterpreting qualitative data can be as damaging as disregarding feedback in traditional evaluation methods, resembling the issues found in the top-down approach, not to mention the subjectivity problem. Mishandling qualitative data throughout the process not only renders the participatory approach ineffective but also leads to unnecessary direct and indirect costs for the organization.

Thirdly, at times, offering opinions within certain organizations may differ from providing constructive criticism. Frequently, convening to express opinions may devolve into mere casual chatter or gossip about various viewpoints. This tendency may be more prevalent in organizations with a specific cultural background, making the participatory process less appealing to management. It can be seen as an opportunity for employees to gather and engage in informal conversations about their superiors or work procedures, often without a clear objective for driving tangible change. On the other hand, certain organizations, despite having dedicated stakeholders with a strong desire to drive innovative change, encounter a challenge where the processes they have initiated are not fully or adequately implemented. This deficiency significantly affects their motivation to participate fully. For instance, even though a participatory process is in place, the allocated budget or the format of the process may not match the significance of the issue that needs to be addressed, ultimately resulting in stakeholders' reluctance to engage wholeheartedly.

The three points mentioned above are just a few examples of the limitations of applying the participatory evaluation model in organizations. In practice, various obstacles and issues can arise, and these may take different forms depending on the social environment and organizational culture. The solution to this matter may not involve selecting just one particular assessment method, but rather, it necessitates an examination of which situations or issues are more suitable for each method. For example, larger organizations may be better equipped to allocate financial resources for participatory processes than smaller organizations. However, the mere availability of financial resources doesn't guarantee that every issue can make use of participatory evaluation methods. Matters of urgent importance may not be conducive to participatory evaluation methods. Additionally, sensitive issues stemming from inherent vulnerabilities may not be appropriate for participatory evaluation models either. Therefore, it can be stated that the most effective approach to implementing a participatory evaluation model is to strike a balance in the level of participation that aligns with the type and nature of the issues at hand. When this balance is achieved successfully, the use of participatory evaluation models can yield the best results and have a meaningful impact.

Concluding Remarks

Participatory Evaluation is one of many valuable evaluation approaches that promote stakeholder engagement, ownership, and empowerment, benefiting organizations by ensuring that all relevant parties are heard and valued. This inclusivity allows organizations to tailor evaluation processes to their unique needs, resulting in more accurate and meaningful results at the individual, organizational, and societal levels.

A key characteristic of this approach is its ability to foster collaboration, transparency, and accountability throughout the process. This leads to balanced and comprehensive evaluations with results that are more likely to be accepted and acted upon. Another significant advantage of Participatory Evaluation is its flexibility, enabling organizations to select suitable evaluation methods and tools that adapt to specific contexts and stakeholders.

Furthermore, as stakeholders reflect on their work, learn from successes and challenges, and make data-driven decisions for future actions, this approach nurtures a culture of learning and continuous improvement. In today's volatile, uncertain, complex, and ambiguous (VUCA) and brittle, anxious, non-linear, and incomprehensible (BANI) context, adaptability and innovation that arise from the process of integrating a participatory approach to overcome persisting challenges are crucial.

However, it's important to remember that there are also disadvantages to participatory assessment. Therefore, organizations must carefully choose the assessment form, seeking a balanced approach to achieve maximum efficiency, effectiveness, and suitability.

References

Aithal, P. S., & Aithal, S. (2023). How to increase emotional infrastructure of higher education institutions. *International Journal of Management, Technology and Social Sciences (IJMTS), 8*(3), 356–394.

AlYahya, M. S., Mat, N. B., & Awadh, A. M. (2013). Review of theory of human resources development training (learning) participation. *Journal of WEI Business and Economics, 2*(1), 47–58.

Barnett, R., & Davis, S. (2008). Creating greater success in succession planning. *Advances in Developing Human Resources, 10*(5), 721–739.

Bennett, E. E., & McWhorter, R. R. (2021). Virtual HRD's role in crisis and the post Covid-19 professional lifeworld: Accelerating skills for digital transformation. *Advances in Developing Human Resources, 23*(1), 5–25.

Bin Othayman, M., Mulyata, J., Meshari, A., & Debrah, Y. (2022). The challenges confronting the training needs assessment in Saudi Arabian higher education. *International Journal of Engineering Business Management, 14*, 18479790211049704.

Bosma, A. R., Boot, C. R., Schaap, R., Schaafsma, F. G., & Anema, J. R. (2022). Participatory approach to create a supportive work environment for employees with chronic conditions: A pilot implementation study. *Journal of Occupational and Environmental Medicine, 64*(8), 665.

Butt, A. S. (2021). Consequences of top-down knowledge hiding: A multi-level exploratory study. *VINE Journal of Information and Knowledge Management Systems, 51*(5), 749–772.

Butterfoss, F. D., Francisco, V., & Capwell, E. M. (2001). Stakeholder participation in evaluation. *Health Promotion Practice, 2*(2), 114–119.

Choi, H. J., & Park, J. H. (2022). Exploring deficiencies in the professional capabilities of novice practitioners to reshape the undergraduate human resource development curriculum in South Korea. *Sustainability, 14*(19), 12121.

Chouinard, J. A. (2013). The case for participatory evaluation in an era of accountability. *American Journal of Evaluation, 34*(2), 237–253.

Chukwu, G. (2015). *Participatory evaluation: An action research intervention to improve training effectiveness* [Doctoral dissertation]. University of Liverpool.

Chukwu, G. M. (2018). Giving 'power to the people' in a Nigerian hospital: From evaluation over to evaluation with stakeholders. *Action Research, 16*(4), 361–375.

Cousins, J. B., & Earl, L. M. (1992). The case for participatory evaluation. *Educational Evaluation and Policy Analysis, 14*(4), 397–418.

Cullen, A., & Coryn, C. L. (2011). Forms and functions of participatory evaluation in international development: A review of the empirical and theoretical literature. *Journal of Multidisciplinary Evaluation, 7*(16), 32–47.

Cullen, A. E., Coryn, C. L., & Rugh, J. (2011). The politics and consequences of including stakeholders in international development evaluation. *American Journal of Evaluation, 32*(3), 345–361.

Doufexi, T., & Pampouri, A. (2022). Evaluation of employees' vocational training programmes and professional development: A case study in Greece. *Journal of Adult and Continuing Education, 28*(1), 49–72.

Erciyes, E. (2020). Paradigms of inquiry in the qualitative research. *European Scientific Journal, ESJ, 16*(7), 181.

Esper, S. C., Barin-Cruz, L., & Gond, J. P. (2023). Engaging stakeholders during intergovernmental conflict: How political attributions shape stakeholder engagement. *Journal of Business Ethics*, 1–27.

Ferguson, L., Chan, S., Santelmann, M., & Tilt, B. (2017). Exploring participant motivations and expectations in a researcher-stakeholder engagement process: Willamette Water 2100. *Landscape and Urban Planning, 157*, 447–456.

Fukuda-Parr, S., & Gibbons, E. (2021). Emerging consensus on 'ethical AI': Human rights critique of stakeholder guidelines. *Global Policy, 12*, 32–44.

Galli, B. J. (2018). Change management models: A comparative analysis and concerns. *IEEE Engineering Management Review, 46*(3), 124–132.
Gasparatos, A., & Scolobig, A. (2012). Choosing the most appropriate sustainability assessment tool. *Ecological Economics, 80*, 1–7.
Guinan, P. J., Parise, S., & Langowitz, N. (2019). Creating an innovative digital project team: Levers to enable digital transformation. *Business Horizons, 62*(6), 717–727.
Hailu, F. (2013). Ethical issues in human resource management practices under federal civil service of Ethiopia the role of human resource practitioner. *International Journal of Research in Commerce & Management, 4*(4), 117–121.
Hasson, H., Villaume, K., von Thiele Schwarz, U., & Palm, K. (2014). Managing implementation. *Journal of Occupational and Environmental Medicine, 56*(1), 58–65.
Joseph-Richard, P., & McCray, J. (2023). Evaluating leadership development in a changing world? Alternative models and approaches for healthcare organisations. *Human Resource Development International, 26*(2), 114–150.
Kemmis, S., & McTaggart, R. (2003). Participatory action research. In N. K. Denzin & Y. S. Lincoln (Eds.), *Strategies of qualitative inquiry* (2nd ed., pp. 336–396). Sage.
Ketola, E., Toropainen, E., Kaila, M., Luoto, R., & Mäkelä, M. (2007). Prioritizing guideline topics: Development and evaluation of a practical tool. *Journal of Evaluation in Clinical Practice, 13*(4), 627–631.
Kibukho, K. (2021). Mediating role of citizen empowerment in the relationship between participatory monitoring and evaluation and social sustainability. *Evaluation and Program Planning, 85*, 101911.
Marion, T. J., & Fixson, S. K. (2021). The transformation of the innovation process: How digital tools are changing work, collaboration, and organizations in new product development. *Journal of Product Innovation Management, 38*(1), 192–215.
McTaggart, R. (1991). Principles for participatory action research. *Adult Education Quarterly, 41*(3), 168.
Meena, A., Dhir, S., & Sushil, S. (2023). Coopetition, strategy, and business performance in the era of digital transformation using a multi-method approach: Some research implications for strategy and operations management. *International Journal of Production Economics*, 109068.
Mlambo, M., Silén, C., & McGrath, C. (2021). Lifelong learning and nurses' continuing professional development, a metasynthesis of the literature. *BMC Nursing, 20*, 1–13.
Nickols, F. W. (2005). Why a stakeholder approach to evaluating training. *Advances in Developing Human Resources, 7*(1), 121–134.
Nielsen, K. (2013). How can we make organizational interventions work? Employees and line managers as actively crafting interventions. *Human Relations, 66*(8), 1029–1050.
Nielsen, K. (2017). Organizational occupational health interventions: What works for whom in which circumstances? *Occupational Medicine, 67*(6), 410–412.
O'Sullivan, R. G., & D'Agostino, A. (2002). Promoting evaluation through collaboration: Findings from community-based programs for young children and their families. *Evaluation, 8*(3), 372–387.
Pollock, A., Campbell, P., Struthers, C., Synnot, A., Nunn, J., Hill, S., Goodare, H., Morris, J., Watts, C., & Morley, R. (2019). Development of the ACTIVE framework to describe stakeholder involvement in systematic reviews. *Journal of Health Services Research & Policy, 24*(4), 245–255.
Roxas, F. M. Y., Rivera, J. P. R., & Gutierrez, E. L. M. (2020). Mapping stakeholders' roles in governing sustainable tourism destinations. *Journal of Hospitality and Tourism Management, 45*, 387–398.
Ryan, K., Greene, J., Lincoln, Y., Mathison, S., Mertens, D. M., & Ryan, K. (1998). Advantages and challenges of using inclusive evaluation approaches in evaluation practice. *American Journal of Evaluation, 19*, 101–122.
Sambhalwal, P., & Kaur, R. (2023). Shifting paradigms in managing organizational change: The evolving role of HR. *Journal of Namibian Studies: History Politics Culture, 33*, 2048–2061.

Shahzad, M., Qu, Y., Zafar, A. U., Ding, X., & Rehman, S. U. (2020). Translating stakeholders' pressure into environmental practices—The mediating role of knowledge management. *Journal of Cleaner Production, 275*, 124163.
Singh, A., Klarner, P., & Hess, T. (2020). How do chief digital officers pursue digital transformation activities? The role of organization design parameters. *Long Range Planning, 53*(3), 101890.
Slotte, V., Tynjälä, P., & Hytönen, T. (2004). How do HRD practitioners describe learning at work? *Human Resource Development International, 7*(4), 481–499.
Song, Y. (2004). Development of learning-oriented evaluation for HRD programs. *ERIC*. Online Submission. Retrieved from https://files.eric.ed.gov/fulltext/ED492300.pdf
Stahl, G. K., Brewster, C. J., Collings, D. G., & Hajro, A. (2020). Enhancing the role of human resource management in corporate sustainability and social responsibility: A multi-stakeholder, multidimensional approach to HRM. *Human Resource Management Review, 30*(3), 100708.
Sthapit, A. (2021). Organisational manoeuvres to manage human resource development strategically: A review of strategic HRD factors. *PYC Nepal Journal of Management, 14*(1), 1–15.
von Thiele Schwarz, U., Nielsen, K., Edwards, K., Hasson, H., Ipsen, C., Savage, C., Abildgaard, J. S., Richter, A., Lornudd, C., Mazzocato, P., & Reed, J. E. (2021). How to design, implement and evaluate organizational interventions for maximum impact: The Sigtuna Principles. *European Journal of Work and Organizational Psychology, 30*(3), 415–427.
Waite, A. M. (2013). Leadership's influence on innovation and sustainability: A review of the literature and implications for HRD. *European Journal of Training and Development, 38*(1/2), 15–39.
Weaver, L., & Cousins, J. B. (2004). Unpacking the participatory process. *Journal of Multidisciplinary Evaluation, 1*(1), 19–40.
Weiss, C. H. (1983). The stakeholder approach to evaluation: Origins and promise. *New Directions for Program Evaluation, 1983*(17), 3–14.
Williams, R. (2020). The paradigm wars: Is MMR really a solution? *American Journal of Trade and Policy, 7*(3), 79–84.

Chapter 8
The Need for an Integrated Evaluation Model

Introduction

Human resource (HR) research is a multifaceted field that encompasses various aspects such as recruitment, training, performance management, and employee well-being. It also involves complex interventions and interventions that occur over a period of time (Brewster et al., 2016). To capture the comprehensive effects of these diverse areas and understand the long-term effects and sustainability of these interventions, an integrated evaluation model allows for a holistic assessment of the outcomes and impacts (Uitto, 2019). The integrated evaluation model considers the interconnectedness and interdependencies between different elements of HR practices and how they collectively contribute to organizational performance and employee satisfaction (Jiang et al., 2013). Also, integrated evaluation model provides a systematic framework for examining the outcomes and impacts at different stages of the research process and enables researchers to track the progress, identify any potential gaps or challenges, and make informed decisions for further improvement (Thiele Schwarz et al., 2016). Furthermore, an integrated evaluation model facilitates the integration of multiple data sources and methodologies because HR research often relies on various data collection methods such as surveys, interviews, observations, and performance metrics. By integrating these diverse sources of information, researchers can obtain a more comprehensive and nuanced understanding of the outcomes and impacts. This approach enhances the validity and reliability of the evaluation findings and enables triangulation of data to strengthen the overall assessment. Additionally, by incorporating a contextual analysis (considering the contextual factors that influence the outcomes and impacts) within the evaluation model, researchers can identify the specific factors that contribute to successful outcomes or hinder desired impacts (Brinkerhoff, 1988). This knowledge is valuable for tailoring HR strategies to different organizational contexts and maximizing their effectiveness.

N. Kiettikunwong and P. Narot, *Determining Outcomes and Impacts of Human Resource Development Programs*, https://doi.org/10.1007/978-981-97-0395-1_8

Potential Benefits of an Integrated Approach

An integrated approach for measuring the outcomes and impacts of HR research offers several significant benefits that contribute to a comprehensive understanding of complex problems. One of the key advantages is the integrated approach provides a holistic view of HR research. It goes beyond isolated measurements of individual variables and considers the broader context in which HR interventions operate. This holistic perspective recognizes that HR outcomes and impacts are influenced by a range of interconnected factors, e.g., organizational culture, leadership practices, external market conditions, and employee engagement (Albrecht et al., 2015).

By embracing this holistic view, researchers can gain a more comprehensive understanding of the versatile nature of HR and its effects on organizational performance and employee well-being. At the same time, integrating contextual analysis within the evaluation framework allows researchers to consider the specific factors that influence HR outcomes and impacts. Different organizations operate in diverse contexts, such as different industries, regions, or cultural settings. By acknowledging and understanding these contextual factors, researchers can tailor their evaluations to account for the unique challenges and opportunities faced by organizations. This contextual sensitivity ensures that the outcomes and impacts measured are relevant, meaningful, and applicable to the specific organizational context, enhancing the validity and applicability of the research findings (Farndale et al., 2023). To illustrate the benefits of an integrated approach for measuring the outcomes and impacts of HR research, let's consider two examples: the implementation of a diversity and inclusion program and the evaluation of a leadership development initiative.

Firstly, let's examine the implementation of a diversity and inclusion program in a multinational organization. An integrated approach would involve considering various perspectives and disciplines, such as sociology, psychology, and organizational behavior, to gain a comprehensive understanding of the program's outcomes and impacts. By taking a holistic view, researchers can go beyond simple diversity metrics and delve deeper into the organizational culture, leadership practices, and employee perceptions and experiences (Shuck, 2011). This approach recognizes that the effectiveness of diversity and inclusion initiatives is not solely measured by the number of diverse hires but also by the extent to which employees feel included, valued, and empowered. By integrating contextual analysis, researchers can consider factors such as regional diversity, cultural norms, and industry-specific challenges, which may influence the outcomes and impacts of the program. This contextual sensitivity allows for tailored evaluations that provide relevant insights and actionable recommendations specific to the organization's unique context (Pless & Maak, 2004).

Now, let's explore the evaluation of a leadership development initiative in a medium-sized company. An integrated approach would involve combining multiple perspectives, such as psychology, human resource management, and organizational development, to assess the outcomes and impacts of the program. Rather than solely focusing on short-term outcomes, such as participant satisfaction or knowledge gain, an integrated approach would consider the long-term impacts on leadership effectiveness, employee engagement, and organizational performance (Benitez et al., 2020). By taking a holistic view, researchers can analyze the interplay between leadership behaviors, organizational culture, and employee outcomes, recognizing that effective leadership extends beyond individual competencies. Integrating contextual analysis would enable researchers to examine how the program's outcomes and impacts differ across departments, levels of management, or geographical locations. This contextual understanding can reveal unique challenges, such as cultural differences or organizational structures, that may influence the effectiveness of the leadership development initiative (Zhu et al., 2004). By capturing both short-term and long-term outcomes and considering the broader context, the evaluation can provide a comprehensive understanding of how the leadership program contributes to organizational success.

In both examples, the integrated approach allows researchers to go beyond simplistic measures and delve into the complexities of HR outcomes and impacts. By embracing a holistic view and incorporating contextual analysis, researchers can gain a deeper understanding of the underlying mechanisms, contributing factors, and potential barriers that influence HR interventions. This comprehensive understanding provides organizations with actionable insights to enhance their strategies, improve decision-making, and maximize the effectiveness of their HR initiatives.

Key Components of the Integrated Evaluation Model

Understanding the components of the integrated evaluation model for measuring the outcomes and impacts of HR research is crucial. By providing a systematic framework, identifying key drivers, capturing interrelationships, and facilitating measurement of short-term and long-term outcomes and impacts, the model enhances the understanding of the complex nature of HR interventions. This understanding enables researchers, practitioners, and policymakers to make evidence-based decisions, design targeted interventions, and improve organizational performance and employee well-being (Alvarez et al., 2004). Ultimately, the components of the evaluation model contribute to the advancement in the realm of HR research and practice, promoting organizational success and fostering positive employee experiences. Upon recognizing the absence of a previously presented model, the author was motivated to develop and subsequently test the proposed framework in real-world settings, aiming to assess its applicability and limitations for future refinement. As a result of the comprehensive study, three key components have emerged that hold substantial influence over human resource development. The three key components are **a long and healthy life**, **education and knowledge**, and **a decent standard of living**. These identified components are considered pivotal in shaping the outcomes and impacts of HR interventions, as they are grounded in the scholarly perspective that comprehensive evaluation frameworks should encompass multiple dimensions of both employee well-being and organizational performance (Roser, 2014).

Consider the first component: **a long and healthy life**. This encompasses the physical and mental well-being of employees. When organizations prioritize the health and well-being of their workforce, they can witness numerous positive outcomes. For instance, implementing wellness programs that encourage exercise, provide access to nutritious meals, and promote stress management can lead to reduced absenteeism, increased employee engagement, and improved overall job satisfaction (Gilbreath & Benson, 2004). By evaluating the impact of HR interventions on employees' long and healthy lives, organizations can gather data on various indicators such as employee stress levels, work-life balance, and job satisfaction. This evaluation allows organizations to identify the effectiveness of their well-being programs and make informed decisions to further enhance the physical and mental health of their workforce (Roser, 2014).

Moving on to the second component: **education and knowledge**. In today's rapidly changing business landscape, continuous learning and knowledge acquisition are crucial for individual and organizational success. Organizations that invest in employee training and development programs foster a culture of learning and innovation. By evaluating the knowledge component, organizations can measure the impact of HR interventions on employees' knowledge acquisition, skill development, and career advancement. This evaluation involves conducting pre- and post-training assessments, gathering feedback from employees and supervisors, and analyzing performance evaluations (Olsson & Gustafsson, 2020). By assessing the impact of HR interventions on knowledge, organizations can identify the effectiveness of their training programs, understand employees' learning needs, and align HR practices with the goal of continuous learning and growth.

Finally, the component of **a decent standard of living**. Employee well-being goes beyond the confines of the workplace; it extends to their economic welfare and overall quality of life. Organizations that strive to ensure fair compensation, provide financial stability, and create opportunities for career growth contribute to the well-being of their employees. By evaluating this component, organizations can assess the impact of their HR interventions on employees' economic well-being. This evaluation involves analyzing data on salary levels, benefits packages, employee satisfaction surveys, and career progression metrics (Stern, 2019). By understanding the impact of HR interventions on a decent standard of living, organizations can create an environment where employees have a reasonable income, financial security, and opportunities for professional advancement. This, in turn, leads to increased employee satisfaction, loyalty, and productivity (Baral & Bhargava, 2011).

Incorporating these three crucial components into the evaluation of HR practices provides organizations with a comprehensive understanding of the outcomes and impacts of their initiatives. It goes beyond mere financial metrics and delves into the holistic well-being of employees. By considering employees' physical and mental health, knowledge and skills, and economic well-being, organizations can tailor their HR strategies to create a supportive and fulfilling work environment. This comprehensive evaluation enables organizations to make informed decisions, foster continuous improvement, and ultimately enhance the overall employee experience.

By recognizing the significance of long and healthy lives, knowledge, and a decent standard of living, organizations can design and implement HR practices that prioritize employee well-being, growth, and satisfaction. This, in turn, leads to a more engaged and productive workforce, higher retention rates, and ultimately contributes to the overall success and sustainability of the organization. Therefore, an integrated approach that incorporates these three components is essential for evaluating the outcomes and impacts of HR research, as it provides organizations with valuable insights to drive continuous improvement and create a work environment that nurtures the well-being and growth of their employees (Gupta, 2014).

A Long and Healthy Life

Human development plays a critical role in enabling individuals to achieve their life goals and realize their potential (Stewart, 2019). Moreover, human resource development is instrumental in attaining globally recognized sustainable development goals, such as poverty eradication, equity, and equal opportunities for all-round development. Consequently, it becomes imperative for countries to formulate strategic plans specifically tailored for human resource development. These plans facilitate the establishment of a clear development process and criteria for evaluating human development outcomes. The assessment results can then be translated into practical measures, rather than remaining confined to theoretical frameworks, thereby enabling the development of human capital—a key determinant of strategic plan success or failure (Le Blanc, 2015).

Scholars, agencies, and government sectors responsible for human resource development (HRD) have endeavored to establish criteria for assessing HRD projects. However, to date, there is no universally applicable criterion for evaluating every project (Lincoln & Lynham, 2011). Recognizing this need, the United Nations Development Programme (UNDP) presents an annual report titled the "Human Development Report," which incorporates the Human Development Index (HDI). The primary objective behind the creation of HDI is to shift the focus away from assessing a country's development solely based on economic growth. Instead, it emphasizes that the people and their capabilities should serve as the ultimate criteria for evaluating a nation's development. Moreover, HDI can be employed to question national policy choices, such as understanding the disparities in HDI levels between two countries with similar Gross National Income (GNI) per capita. These disparities shed light on how different countries prioritize their policy choices at the national level (Ghislandi et al., 2019).

The HDI serves as a widely recognized standard criterion for measuring a country's success in human resource development. It comprises three main aspects: long and healthy life, education and knowledge, and a decent standard of living. Among these, living a "long and healthy life" holds utmost importance in human development as individuals can fully develop and contribute when they are physically and mentally robust. However, it is essential to note that although HDI is a significant and standardized indicator, it merely represents a geometric mean divided into various dimensions. Consequently, it poses challenges when attempting to translate HDI results into practical measures for human development (Chulanova et al., 2019).

Universally, the term "health" encompasses the perfect state of human beings in their physical, mental, social, and intellectual dimensions. These aspects are interconnected and require a balanced integration in order to achieve holistic human development. Recognizing this, assessors have identified four distinct dimensions for the purpose of health assessment:

1. The physical aspect refers to overall physical well-being, including factors such as physical fitness, work capacity, access to healthcare, and sanitation.
2. The mental aspect involves individuals' attitudes towards maintaining good health and well-being.
3. The social aspect relates to individuals' abilities to effectively communicate, provide support, and care for others, thereby fostering the development of friendships, unity, problem-solving skills, and personal growth. It also emphasizes the importance of contributing to society and the environment while adhering to social norms and legal frameworks.
4. The spiritual aspect entails the acquisition of knowledge, encompassing both professional knowledge and the continual pursuit of new knowledge. Moreover, it emphasizes the practical application of acquired knowledge to solve problems and address challenges.

These dimensions provide a comprehensive framework for assessing the various aspects of health, allowing for a more nuanced understanding of individuals' overall well-being. In the subsequent sections, further details regarding the spiritual aspect will be elaborated upon.

Education and Knowledge

In the past, traditional teaching methods characterized by lecture-based and teacher-centered approaches were prevalent in classrooms worldwide. These methods primarily focused on memorization through rote learning, with limited emphasis on fostering creativity and self-development at all levels of education. While it is important to acknowledge that educators during that era made some positive contributions to student development, it is evident that such teaching practices are no longer suitable in the digital age. In this era of technological advancement and global competition, digital intervention has profoundly influenced every aspect of development.

It is crucial to distinguish between education and knowledge: education refers to the process of how knowledge is acquired, while knowledge represents what one knows. Both education and knowledge are vital components of HRD. An effective education system should aim to enhance learners' abilities to seek and apply knowledge from diverse sources to appropriately solve problems. Learning should

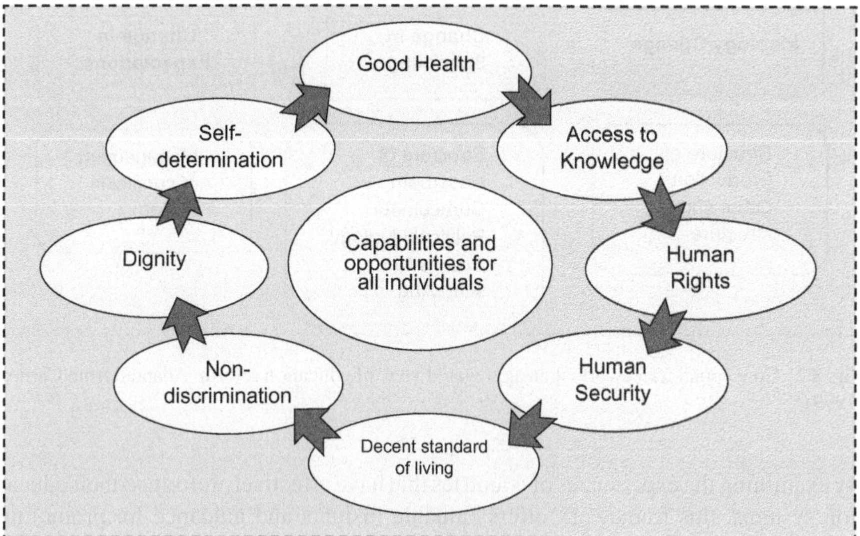

Fig. 8.1 Human development for everyone. Adapted from Infographic 1 Human development for everyone, Human Development Report 2016 by UNDP

be viewed as an ongoing process with no limitations or boundaries in terms of time, space, and methods. This approach allows for continuous enhancement and expansion of knowledge and skills (Shin et al., 2020).

In addition to physical development, the intellectual aspect of human development is equally significant, particularly in breaking the cycle of poverty. Encouraging intellectual development alongside physical development through education proves to be more efficient. This concept aligns with the Human Development Index (HDI) developed by the United Nations, as illustrated in Fig. 8.1 (United Nations Development Programme, 2016).

To effectively reform the education system, it is essential to establish clear and comprehensive operational strategies that provide explicit guidelines for transforming traditional education into a system that fully supports learners' holistic development throughout their lives. Developed countries, such as the United States of America, the United Kingdom, Germany, Japan, South Korea, and Singapore, have consistently prioritized human resource development. Their substantial investments in human development have resulted in rapid and sustainable progress. Notably, these countries have successfully reformed their education systems, as evidenced by their high rates of educated populations (Prata et al., 2010).

Drawing upon a systematic synthesis of concepts and models derived from the successful education reforms in these countries, an integrated perspective on education reform has been developed. This perspective serves as a framework for assessing research projects and formulating policies aimed at enhancing education.

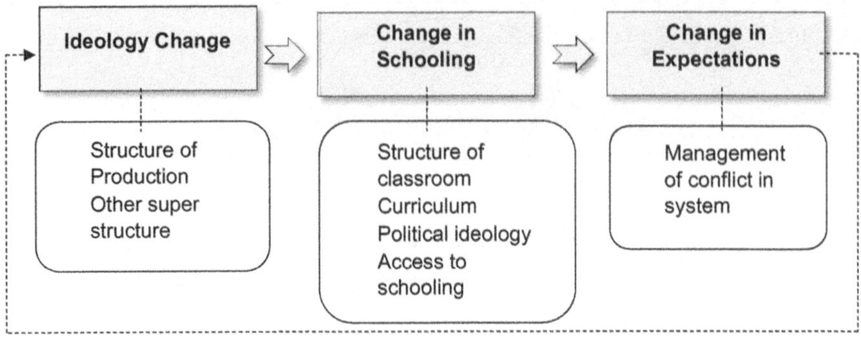

Fig. 8.2 Conceptual framework of an aggregated view of education reform. Adapted from Carnoy (1999)

By examining the experiences of countries that have effectively reformed their education systems, this framework offers valuable insights and guidance for promoting educational improvement on a broader scale (Verger et al., 2016).

In summary, establishing explicit guidelines and adopting a comprehensive approach to education reform is crucial. Learning from the experiences of countries that have achieved successful education reforms allows for the formulation of effective strategies and policies to enhance education systems worldwide (Fig. 8.2).

Based on the aforementioned framework, the process of effective education reform should proceed in an orderly and systematic manner, encompassing three stages: "Ideology Change," "Change in Schooling," and "Change in Expectations." Each stage involves key variables that can be summarized as follows:

Ideology change:

- Structure of production: This refers to the formal structure within the education system that is vital for driving educational reform in Thailand, including budgeting, allocation of public resources for education, educational personnel, and related laws and regulations.
- Other superstructures: These encompass other essential structures that are not part of the formal production structure but have an informal and flexible relationship with it. Superstructures such as culture, political power, state power, family, and religions often influence the structure of production as they form part of society's fabric and serve as its foundation.

Change in schooling:

- Structure of classroom: This pertains to the physical environment of classrooms. Modifying the classroom environment can foster effective learning and prevent behavioral issues that may hinder learning. An optimal classroom environment should encourage learners to express themselves, foster a sense of belonging, and discover their hidden talents and abilities.

- Curriculum: This refers to the content and lessons taught in schools or educational institutions. It encompasses learning standards, educational objectives, learning units and lessons, student assignments and projects, learning materials, testing and assessment methods, and other means of evaluating student performance and learning.
- Political ideology: This involves political ideas and beliefs, particularly those related to objectives and methods for achieving different goals within each political ideology. It includes shifting from "Conservatism," which aims to preserve traditional social institutions and slow down the modernization process, to "Liberalism," which emphasizes individual liberty and limits the government's role through decentralization, such as decentralizing education systems.
- Access to schooling: This factor, crucial for the HDI, denotes equal educational opportunities for all individuals, regardless of their social status, gender, race, or physical and mental disabilities. It also encompasses designing school strategies and policies to eliminate intentional or unintentional barriers to students' academic achievements.

Change in expectations:

- Management of conflict in the system: This involves handling conflicts that arise during the implementation of educational policies and reforms, as various limitations and conflicts can impact the success or failure of education reform efforts. For example, issues related to the distribution of public resources and the ability to affect political ideology change may pose challenges. Hence, it is vital to consider potential obstacles to education reform, promote awareness and understanding, and seek democratic solutions.

Overall, understanding and addressing these components within each stage of the reform process are critical for successful education reform initiatives.

A Decent Standard of Living

While there may be a process of physical and intellectual development for the workforce, no matter how effective it may be, it would be in vain if those workers are unable to utilize their enhanced potential to improve their social status. In other words, investing in these two components alone would yield limited results. To identify the crucial points to evaluate the final key component of a decent standard of living, which can be simplified as increased opportunities for economic advancement, several statistics are used to measure inequality, such as the Gini coefficient, which quantifies income inequality, and Theil-L, a useful tool for studying economic phenomena and factors that contribute to economic inequality. However, measuring poverty and income inequality alone might not be sufficient to examine opportunities for economic advancement, as there are other factors that should be taken into consideration. Therefore, to ensure measurement accuracy, social mobility should also be examined. In societies with high levels of economic inequality, the opportunity for economic advancement tends to be limited, while equal opportunities for all individuals result in increased opportunities for households to improve their economic status. In general, households can be categorized into five types based on their wealth:

Poor—Average per capita income falls below the 20th percentile.
Relatively poor—Average per capita income ranges from the 21st to the 40th percentile.
Middle income—Average per capita income ranges from the 41st to the 60th percentile.
Relatively wealthy—Average per capita income ranges from the 61st to the 80th percentile.
Wealthy—Average per capita income exceeds the 81st percentile.

Offering equal opportunities is crucial for economic growth because if economic development aims to provide opportunities for upward mobility, households have a better chance to improve their status regardless of their initial income. Therefore, it is also necessary to measure other factors that affect the economic growth of the poor, as they reveal opportunities for improving economic status. One recommended measurement method by the World Bank is assessing the pro-poorness of growth, such as using the Growth Incidence Curve (GIC) developed by Ferreira (2010).

The GIC measures the annualized growth rate of per capita income for each percentile of the income distribution between two points in time. The results from the GIC indicate whether the national economic growth benefits the poor or not. The GIC is calculated using data on income inequality collected from Household Socio-Economic Surveys (SES), which include information on income, debt, occupation, education, financial access, and residential area (Ravallion & Chen, 2003).

Apart from the GIC, Gross National Income (GNI) per capita is also an indicator of the social, economic, and environmental well-being of a country and its people. For example, countries with above-average per capita income generally have longer life expectancy, lower infant mortality, higher literacy rates, and better access to clean water. Thus, measuring GNI provides insights into a country's strength, competitiveness, economic needs, and general living standards of its citizens. GNI accounts for both national income and net income received from abroad, while Gross Domestic Product (GDP) only calculates income generated within the domestic economy. GNI is derived by combining GDP and net income received from overseas (Capelli & Vaggi, 2013) (Fig. 8.3).

Therefore, the measurement of an opportunity to improve economic status can be conducted by examining two primary aspects: (1) the opportunity for economic mobility, which can be quantified using the Growth Incidence Curve, and (2) the

$$GNI = GDP + (\$\, flowing\ from\ foreign\ countries - \$ flowing\ to\ foreign\ countries)$$

Fig. 8.3 Formula for calculating Gross National Income per capita

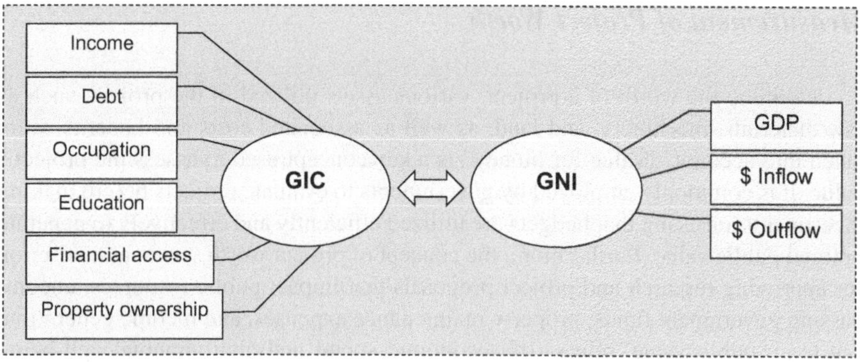

Fig. 8.4 Framework to assess opportunity for economic status improvement

strength and competitiveness in the global market, which indicates the extent to which laborers are afforded opportunities for economic advancement. Considering these factors, a conceptual framework for opportunity assessment has been developed and is illustrated in Fig. 8.4.

Influencing Contextual Factors on the Outcomes and Impacts of HR Research

In addition to the three key components and suggested minor points that should be considered when conducting an evaluation, there are also influencing contextual factors that should be taken into account when evaluating the outcomes and impacts of HR research. The following are secondary factors that may have an influence.

Content Coverage and Coherence of the Projects

To examine the content coverage and coherence between sub-projects and the main project within the project series related to human resource development in Thailand, a content analysis and classification were conducted by the assessors. The structure of the main content was established based on the previously presented conceptual frameworks, followed by the identification of sub-content. Subsequently, a systematic analysis and interpretation of the content were performed, drawing upon concepts and knowledge obtained from a literature review, in order to assess the extent of content coverage and coherence across the projects.

Measurement of Project Worth

To determine the worth of a project, various assets utilized in the project, such as raw materials, machinery, and land, as well as associated costs and benefits, were taken into account. "Value for money" is a key concept used to assess the project's value. It is commonly employed by governments to evaluate projects before making investments, ensuring that budgets are utilized efficiently and effectively to generate optimal public value. Furthermore, the concept of project worth serves as a criterion for approving research and project proposals that impact public resources, encompassing government funds, property maintenance expenses, and income generation. The term "public value" refers to the economic, social, and environmental well-being of the public. The worth of a project can be measured along three dimensions: (1) Economy, (2) Efficiency, and (3) Effectiveness, as depicted in Fig. 8.5.

Even though measuring the relationship between public resources and public values by the government is a complex process, it can be accomplished by comparing the expenses allocated to public resources with the anticipated or actual public value derived from a specific project. It is important for assessors to recognize that the project's impacts on different social groups may vary. Therefore, to enhance the accuracy of measurement, tools such as cost-effectiveness analysis were employed, which include:

1. Payback Period (PB)
2. Net Present Value (NPV)
3. Internal Rate of Return (IRR)
4. Benefit-to-Cost (B/C) ratio.

These tools enable a comprehensive evaluation of the project's worth, taking into account factors such as the time it takes to recoup investments (PB), the present value of future cash flows (NPV), the rate of return on investment (IRR), and the comparison of project benefits to costs (B/C ratio). By employing these measures, a more robust assessment of the project's cost-effectiveness and its contribution to public value can be achieved.

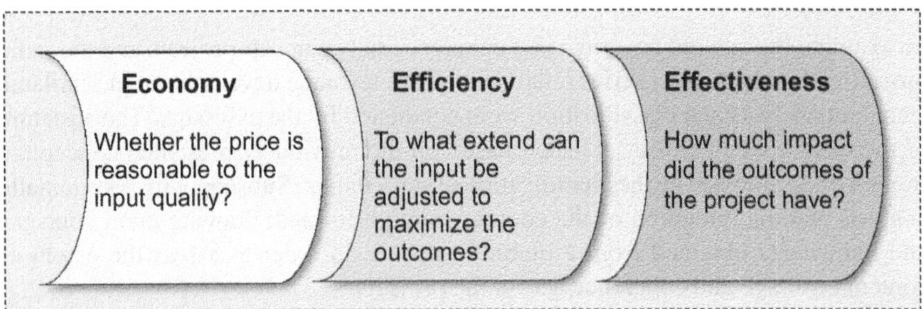

Fig. 8.5 Three-dimension framework to measure the project worth

Evaluation of Project Impact

The measurement of project impact involves analyzing the process by which inputs are transformed into outcomes that yield public value. Through impact analysis, valuable insights can be gained regarding the project's results, thereby informing future projects. To assess project impacts, it is crucial to demonstrate the practicality of implementation. In other words, the projects should be feasible and capable of being effectively executed and sustained. This evaluation encompasses the examination of policy coherence for practical implementation and the assessment of project sustainability, as illustrated in Fig. 8.6.

Figure 8.6 presented outlines four essential components utilized for analyzing the impact of the project. These components are as follows:

1. Logistics: This component involves examining the project outcomes, including the coordination process among various stakeholders and the appropriate utilization of facilities, tools, and materials. The aim is to ensure optimal results through careful resource management.
2. Localism: This component focuses on outcomes that consider the specific contexts of the research areas and embrace a bottom-up approach to management.
3. Legitimacy: This component emphasizes that the project outcomes comply with existing laws and regulations. They are implemented in a manner consistent with the legal framework without disrupting the overall legal system.
4. Performance: This component pertains to outcomes that exemplify best practices, supported by empirical evidence.

A thorough analysis of these elements is necessary to understand their interconnections and the mutual support they provide.

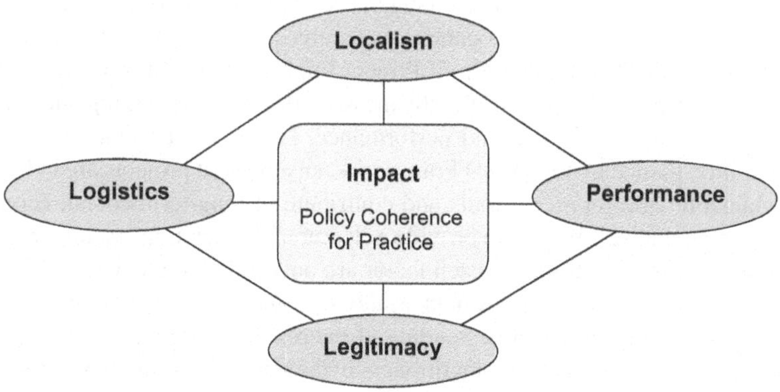

Fig. 8.6 Conceptual framework for project impact evaluation

Evaluation of Project Sustainability

Finally, to assess the sustainability of the project, the assessors utilized the Policy Coherence for Sustainable Development (PCSD) Framework developed by the OECD. This framework serves as a comprehensive tool for analyzing and monitoring the project's progress in relation to the Sustainable Development Goals (SDGs). The SDGs encompass a series of open-ended questions that help elucidate the roles of policymakers, government sectors, the state, government legal departments, and other relevant stakeholders involved in the project's development. They are employed to investigate policies, organizational structures, and the policy-making process, as well as examine the factors that influence the achievement of sustainable development goals. Moreover, the PCSD Framework enables assessors to examine an organization's internal mechanisms and protocols that enhance policy coherence. In the event of any identified incoherence, the framework provides guidance on establishing procedures to ensure that policy implementation aligns with the 2030 Agenda for sustainable development (Shawoo et al., 2022).

From the aforementioned discussion, it can be concluded that a comprehensive evaluation of research projects on human resource development should consider the three essential components: a long and healthy life, education and knowledge, and a decent standard of living. To ensure a holistic assessment, it is also crucial to take into account the Influencing Contextual Factors that impact the outcomes and impacts of HR research. These factors encompass Content Coverage and Coherence of the Projects, Measurement of Project Worth, Evaluation of Project Impact, and Evaluation of Project Sustainability.

By considering these factors, a more comprehensive and nuanced assessment can be conducted. Content Coverage and Coherence of the Projects enables the evaluation of how well the projects align with the defined conceptual frameworks and contribute to the desired outcomes. The Measurement of Project Worth provides insights into the value for money and efficient allocation of resources, ensuring that public funds are utilized effectively. The Evaluation of Project Impact allows for a thorough understanding of the practicality and effectiveness of the projects, taking into account logistics, localism, legitimacy, and performance. Lastly, the Evaluation of Project Sustainability, guided by the PCSD Framework, ensures that projects are in line with the Sustainable Development Goals and contribute to long-term social, economic, and environmental well-being. To provide a clearer understanding, specific examples of assessment considerations for each factor are outlined in Table 8.1.

By incorporating these assessment issues into the evaluation process, a more holistic and comprehensive understanding of the research projects can be achieved. Researchers, policymakers, and practitioners in the field of human resource development can utilize these assessment issues as a guide to assess the projects' outcomes and impacts. Ultimately, such a holistic evaluation approach will contribute to evidence-based decision-making and the development of effective interventions and policies in the field of human resource development.

Table 8.1 Components/factors and evaluation issues for assessment

Components/factors	Evaluation issues
A long and healthy life	• Does the research project contribute to improving healthcare access, quality, and outcomes? • Are there measurable improvements in health indicators, such as life expectancy, mortality rates, disease prevalence, and healthcare utilization? • How effectively does the project address social determinants of health, such as socio-economic factors, environmental conditions, and lifestyle choices?
Education and knowledge	• To what extent does the research project enhance access to education and knowledge for individuals or communities? • Are there improvements in educational infrastructure, curriculum development, or teaching methodologies? • Does the project promote lifelong learning, skill development, and capacity building?
Decent standard of living	• How does the research project contribute to economic development and poverty reduction? • Are there improvements in income levels, employment opportunities, and economic indicators? • Does the project address socio-economic inequalities and promote social inclusion?
Content coverage and coherence of the projects	• Are the research projects aligned with the goals and objectives related to a long and healthy life, education and knowledge, and a decent standard of living? • Is the content of the projects comprehensive and adequately covers the key aspects of human resource development? • Is there coherence and consistency among the sub-projects within the project series?
Measurement of project worth	• How effectively are the resources, such as raw materials, machinery, and wages, utilized in the projects? • Is the project demonstrating value for money by efficiently utilizing the allocated budget to generate public value? • Have cost-effectiveness analysis tools, such as payback period, net present value, internal rate of return, and B/C ratio, been utilized to assess the worth of the project?

(continued)

Table 8.1 (continued)

Components/factors	Evaluation issues
Evaluation of project impact	• How have the research projects contributed to the promotion of a long and healthy life, education and knowledge, and a decent standard of living? • What are the observed outcomes and impacts resulting from the projects? • Have the projects been practical and feasible to implement, and have they demonstrated performance based on empirical evidence?
Evaluation of project sustainability	• Have the research projects demonstrated policy coherence for sustainable development, considering the SDGs framework? • How well do the projects align with the 2030 agenda of sustainable development? • Is there a clear mechanism in place to address any incoherence found and ensure the long-term sustainability of the projects?

Conclusion

We have presented The Integrated Evaluation Model for Determining Outcomes and Impacts of Human Resource Research, which encompasses three main components: a long and healthy life, education and knowledge, and a decent standard of living. These components are crucial indicators of human development and well-being. Through the examination of sub-components or influencing contextual factors, we have established a comprehensive framework for evaluating human resource research projects. The assessment of content coverage and coherence of the projects ensures that they align with the defined conceptual frameworks and contribute to the desired outcomes. Additionally, the measurement of project worth provides insights into the value for money and the efficient allocation of public resources. The evaluation of project impact allows us to gauge the effectiveness of interventions and assess their practicality in creating tangible results. By considering logistics, localism, legitimacy, and performance, we can better understand the overall impact of the projects and identify areas for improvement. Lastly, the evaluation of project sustainability, based on the Policy Coherence for Sustainable Development (PCSD) Framework, ensures that projects are in line with the Sustainable Development Goals (SDGs) and contribute to long-term social, economic, and environmental well-being. This analysis helps policymakers and stakeholders identify internal mechanisms, protocols, and procedures that enhance policy coherence and align with the 2030 Agenda for sustainable development (OECD, 2016). The Integrated Evaluation Model for Determining Outcomes and Impacts of Human Resource Research presented as shown in Fig. 8.7.

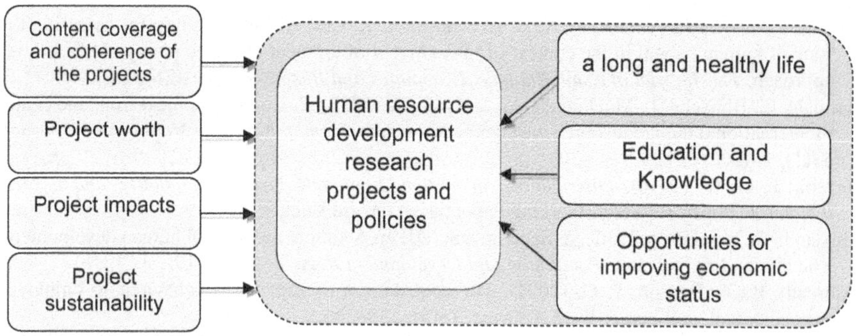

Fig. 8.7 The integrated evaluation model for determining outcomes and impacts of human resource research

Overall, the Integrated Evaluation Model presented in this study provides a comprehensive framework for assessing the outcomes and impacts of human resource research projects. By considering multiple dimensions and contextual factors, it enables a holistic evaluation that considers the diverse aspects of human development and contributes to evidence-based decision-making. We hope that this model will serve as a valuable tool for researchers, policymakers, and practitioners in the field of human resource development, ultimately leading to more effective and impactful interventions and policies.

References

Albrecht, S. L., Bakker, A. B., Gruman, J. A., Macey, W. H., & Saks, A. M. (2015). Employee engagement, human resource management practices and competitive advantage: An integrated approach. *Journal of Organizational Effectiveness: People and Performance.*

Alvarez, K., Salas, E., & Garofano, C. M. (2004). An integrated model of training evaluation and effectiveness. *Human Resource Development Review, 3*(4), 385–416.

Baral, R., & Bhargava, S. (2011). HR interventions for work-life balance: Evidences from organisations in India. *International Journal of Business, Management and Social Sciences, 2*(1), 33–42.

Benitez, G. B., Ayala, N. F., & Frank, A. G. (2020). Industry 4.0 innovation ecosystems: An evolutionary perspective on value cocreation. *International Journal of Production Economics, 228*, 107735.

Brewster, C., Houldsworth, E., Sparrow, P., & Vernon, G. (2016). *International human resource management*. Kogan Page Publishers.

Brinkerhoff, R. O. (1988). An integrated evaluation model for HRD. *Training & Development Journal, 42*(2), 66–69.

Capelli, C., & Vaggi, G. (2013). *A better indicator of standards of living: The Gross National Disposable Income* (DEM Working Papers Series No. 062). University of Pavia, Department of Economics and Management, Pavia.

Carnoy, M. (1999). *Globalization and Educational Reform: What Planners Need to Know*. Retrieved from: https://unesdoc.unesco.org/ark:/48223/pf0000120274

Chulanova, Z. K., Satybaldin, A. A., & Koshanov, A. K. (2019). Methodology for assessing the state of human capital in the context of innovative development of the economy: A three-level approach. *The Journal of Asian Finance, Economics and Business, 6*(1), 321–328.
Farndale, E., Bonache, J., McDonnell, A., & Kwon, B. (2023). Positioning context front and center in international human resource management research. *Human Resource Management Journal, 33*(1), 1–16.
Ferreira, F. H. G. (2010). *Distributions in motion. Economic growth, inequality, and poverty dynamics* (Policy Research Working Paper 5424). World Bank.
Ghislandi, S., Sanderson, W. C., & Scherbov, S. (2019). A simple measure of human development: The human life indicator. *Population and Development Review, 45*(1), 219.
Gilbreath, B., & Benson, P. G. (2004). The contribution of supervisor behaviour to employee psychological well-being. *Work & Stress, 18*(3), 255–266.
Gupta, S. (2014). Sustainability as a competitive advantage: An outcome of strategic HRM. *Review of HRM, 3*, 129–139.
Jiang, K., Takeuchi, R., & Lepak, D. P. (2013). Where do we go from here? New perspectives on the black box in strategic human resource management research. *Journal of Management Studies, 50*(8), 1448–1480.
Le Blanc, D. (2015). Towards integration at last? The sustainable development goals as a network of targets. *Sustainable Development, 23*(3), 176–187.
Lincoln, Y. S., & Lynham, S. A. (2011). Criteria for assessing theory in human resource development from an interpretive perspective. *Human Resource Development International, 14*(1), 3–22.
OECD. (2016). Aligning policy coherence for development to the 2030 agenda. In *Better policies for sustainable development 2016: A new framework for policy coherence*. OECD Publishing.
Olsson, S., & Gustafsson, C. (2020). Employees' experiences of education and knowledge in intellectual disability practice. *Journal of Policy and Practice in Intellectual Disabilities, 17*(3), 219–231.
Pless, N., & Maak, T. (2004). Building an inclusive diversity culture: Principles, processes and practice. *Journal of Business Ethics, 54*, 129–147.
Prata, N., Passano, P., Sreenivas, A., & Gerdts, C. E. (2010). Maternal mortality in developing countries: Challenges in scaling-up priority interventions. *Women's Health, 6*(2), 311–327.
Ravallion, M., & Chen, S. (2003). Measuring pro-poor growth. *Economics Letters, 78*(1), 93–99.
Roser, M. (2014). Human development index (HDI). *Our World in Data*.
Shawoo, Z., Maltais, A., Dzebo, A., & Pickering, J. (2022). Political drivers of policy coherence for sustainable development: An analytical framework. *Environmental Policy and Governance*, 1–12.
Shin, J. C., Li, X., Byun, B. K., & Nam, I. (2020). Building a coordination system of HRD, research and industry for knowledge and technology-driven economic development in South Asia. *International Journal of Educational Development, 74*, 102161.
Shuck, B. (2011). Integrative literature review: Four emerging perspectives of employee engagement: An integrative literature review. *Human Resource Development Review, 10*(3), 304–328.
Stern, G. R. (2019). Healthy workplace connections. *Journal of the American Psychiatric Nurses Association, 25*(3), 218–219.
Stewart, F. (2019). The human development approach: An overview. *Oxford Development Studies, 47*(2), 135–153.
Thiele Schwarz, U., Lundmark, R., & Hasson, H. (2016). The dynamic integrated evaluation model (DIEM): Achieving sustainability in organizational intervention through a participatory evaluation approach. *Stress and Health, 32*(4), 285–293.
Uitto, J. I. (2019). Sustainable development evaluation: Understanding the nexus of natural and human systems. *New Directions for Evaluation, 2019*(162), 49–67.
UNDP (United Nations Development Programme). (2016). *Human development report 2016: Human development for everyone*. UNDP.
Verger, A., Fontdevila, C., & Zancajo, A. (2016). *The privatization of education: A political economy of global education reform*. Teachers College Press.
Zhu, W., May, D. R., & Avolio, B. J. (2004). The impact of ethical leadership behavior on employee outcomes: The roles of psychological empowerment and authenticity. *Journal of Leadership & Organizational Studies, 11*(1), 16–26.

Chapter 9
Methodological Framework for Evaluating Human Resource Research

Introduction

In line with the progressive trajectory of this book, the current chapter serves as a vital conduit between the theoretical foundations and the practical implementation of the Integrated Evaluation Model for determining outcomes and impacts of human resource research. While the preceding chapter (Chap. 5) highlighted the significance of adopting such a model, this chapter takes a deeper dive into the evaluation process, specifically focusing on the methodology employed. By delving into the intricacies of the evaluation methodology, this chapter aims to provide readers with a comprehensive understanding of the practical steps involved in assessing the projects, activities, and impacts related to human resource research. The methodology employed in this evaluation process is designed to address the inherent challenges posed by the vast scope and complexity of human development goals. A key aspect of the methodology is the establishment of a well-structured research design that encompasses appropriate approaches tailored to mature projects. This ensures that the evaluation process is systematic, rigorous, and aligned with the objectives of the research intervention. By studying the strategic plan for economy and development, with a particular focus on human resource development and related policies and activities, the evaluation aims to assess the extent to which the projects have achieved the indicators and goals specified in their plans based on the Integrated Evaluation Model for determining outcomes and impacts of human resource research (Khalife & Hamzeh, 2019).

To gather comprehensive data for evaluation, a mixed-method approach is employed, combining both qualitative and quantitative data collection and analysis. This approach enhances the reliability, validity, and credibility of the data through triangulation (Creswell et al., 2014). The results derived from this analysis are then interpreted to provide profound suggestions and recommendations that reflect the contextual realities and rational considerations. By elucidating the methodology employed in the evaluation process, this chapter equips readers with the necessary insights and tools to navigate the practical aspects of implementing the Integrated

N. Kiettikunwong and P. Narot, *Determining Outcomes and Impacts of Human Resource Development Programs*, https://doi.org/10.1007/978-981-97-0395-1_9

Evaluation Model. It serves as a crucial bridge between the theoretical foundations discussed earlier and the forthcoming chapter (Chap. 7), which will showcase the model's effectiveness in evaluating the outcomes and impacts of human resource research in real-life contexts.

The chapter begins by outlining the key principles and theoretical frameworks that inform the evaluation process. It delves into the various approaches and techniques utilized to gather relevant data and information, ensuring a comprehensive and holistic assessment of the research outcomes and impacts.

Furthermore, the chapter discusses the process of defining evaluation criteria and indicators specific to human resource research. It explores the considerations and factors that inform the selection and development of these criteria, emphasizing their alignment with the fundamental components of a long and healthy life, education and knowledge, and a decent standard of living. The chapter also highlights the importance of incorporating Influencing Contextual Factors, such as content coverage and coherence of projects, measurement of project worth, evaluation of project impact, and evaluation of project sustainability, into the evaluation methodology.

Finally, the chapter provides insights into the practical implementation of the evaluation methodology. It discusses the steps involved in data collection, analysis, and interpretation, ensuring transparency and rigor throughout the process. Additionally, it addresses potential challenges and limitations that may arise during the evaluation and proposes strategies to mitigate them.

Approaches Utilized for Evaluation

To test the viability of the author's evaluation model and explore its strengths, weaknesses, and potential improvements, the authors seized an opportunity to evaluate a series of research projects. These projects were part of a larger initiative focused on human resource development aimed at enhancing workforce competitiveness at the regional level. The research funding for these projects was provided by a government agency responsible for funding such initiatives. By incorporating the proposed model from this book, the authors adhered to the evaluation framework set forth by the research funding agency.

The evaluation process commences with a meticulous analysis of comprehensive project reports, aiming to extensively scrutinize diverse facets of the projects and their resulting outcomes. Through this analysis, evaluators gain insights into how well the projects align with their objectives, activities, and intended outcomes. This assessment allows for an evaluation of the projects' effectiveness in addressing the research goals and targets outlined in their plans (Bottrill & Pressey, 2012). Additionally, the evaluation process includes an assessment of the projects' worth. This assessment considers factors such as the resources invested in the projects, including raw materials, machinery, land, and wages. By comparing the costs incurred with the benefits and outcomes achieved, evaluators can evaluate the projects' value for money. This assessment plays a crucial role in ensuring the efficient and effective utilization of allocated resources, thereby maximizing the public value generated. Furthermore, the evaluation involves a thorough examination of the projects' impacts. This examination entails assessing the effects and consequences of the projects on the target population and the broader society. To gather comprehensive data for this assessment, fieldwork data is collected through in-depth interviews with key stakeholders intimately involved in the projects (Johnson & Rowlands, 2012). These stakeholders encompass project directors, researchers, responsible individuals, and active participants. The insights obtained through these interviews shed light on various aspects, including project implementation, encountered challenges, achieved outcomes, and the overall impact on intended beneficiaries and stakeholders.

To streamline the evaluation process, the projects are categorized into two main groups: human resource research projects that prioritize promoting a healthy lifestyle, and projects that focus on education and knowledge without a specific emphasis on human resource research geared towards improving the living standards of the workforce. This categorization allows for a targeted evaluation within distinct domains, facilitating a more nuanced analysis of the projects' outcomes and impacts. By adopting this approach, evaluators can tailor their assessment strategies to align with the unique characteristics and objectives associated with each category (Stufflebeam, 2000).

Evaluation Objectives

In order to effectively capture the projects' activities and their impact on recipients and stakeholders in relation to the research intervention targets, conducting evaluations becomes a complex task due to the extensive scope and intricacy of human development goals. To address this challenge, a well-structured research design was implemented, incorporating suitable approaches for mature projects (Angel et al., 2000). The evaluation process focused on examining the strategic plan for economic and development purposes, particularly in the realm of human resource development and associated policies and activities. Its primary objective was to assess the extent to which the projects on human resource development successfully achieved the indicators and goals outlined in their plans. This comprehensive examination encompassed projects and activities carried out between 2012 and 2015, aiming to gain insights into their progress, challenges, obstacles, outcomes, and broader effects on the labor sector and society at large. At the core of this evaluation was the assessment of outcomes and impacts of a human resource research program, comprising diverse sub-projects within the overarching research program (Wirtz & Müller, 2021).

Content Wise

The evaluation sought to investigate the strategic plan for economic and development purposes, specifically honing in on policies and activities related to human resource development. Its primary goal was to ascertain the extent to which the projects dedicated to human resource development effectively realized the indicators and goals delineated in their plans. Spanning projects and activities carried out from 2012 to 2015, the evaluation scrutinized their advancement, encountered challenges, prevailing obstacles, achieved outcomes, and the resultant impact on the labor sector and society as a collective entity (Di Baldassarre et al., 2019).

Target Population

The target population was divided into two levels:
Micro-level data: This category involved the collection of data from two distinct population groups. Firstly, laborers were chosen utilizing multi-stage sampling methodologies. Secondly, individuals connected to the projects participated in focus group discussions.

Macro-level data: This comprised both quantitative and qualitative data. Quantitative data were gathered from the affiliated working units and organizations identified in the strategic plan. Qualitative data were acquired through comprehensive interviews with responsible individuals from each project, representing various working units.

Assessment Methodology

In order to obtain comprehensive and reliable data, a mixed-method approach was utilized in the assessment process. This approach involved the collection and analysis of both qualitative and quantitative data, ensuring the reliability, validity, and credibility of the data through data triangulation. The results obtained through this approach were then interpreted to offer meaningful suggestions and recommendations that accurately and logically reflected the context. The specific details of the assessment methodology, based on the framework, are illustrated in the subsequent section (Vandenberg & Lance, 2000).

Evaluation Procedures

The evaluations were conducted systematically by analyzing complete secondary sources within the evaluation framework provided by the research funding agency and other's own. This framework encompassed three key components namely a long and healthy life, education and knowledge, and a decent standard of living and four main critical factors include: (1) the coverage of research content and coherence of the projects; (2) the worth of the projects; (3) the impacts of the projects; and (4) the sustainability of the projects. In addition to the data collected from project reports, fieldwork data was gathered through in-depth interviews with project directors, researchers, responsible individuals, and participants involved in the projects. The projects were categorized into two major groups: human resource development and educational system development.

Content Coverage and Coherence of the Projects

To examine the content coverage and coherence between the sub-projects and the main project within the series of human resource development projects and policies in Thailand, the assessors conducted content analysis and classification. The structure of the main content was established based on the earlier presented conceptual framework, and the sub-content was identified accordingly. The content was then systematically analyzed and interpreted, drawing upon concepts and knowledge derived from the literature review, to assess the extent of content coverage and coherence within the projects (Veltri et al., 2011).

Measurement of the Project's Worth

To determine the worth of a project, various assets utilized in the project, such as raw materials, machinery, land, and wages, were taken into consideration. The costs and benefits of the project were compared to assess its value for money, which is a key concept in measuring the project's worth. Value for money analysis is commonly employed by governments to ensure efficient and effective utilization of budget and creation of optimal public value. The concept of project worth is also an essential criterion in evaluating research and project proposals that involve public resources, including government funds, property maintenance expenses, and income generation. Public value, encompassing economic, social, and environmental well-being, is a defining aspect of project worth and evaluation. The project's worth can be assessed through three dimensions: economy, efficiency, and effectiveness (Lakner & Milanovic, 2013; Aliverdi et al., 2013).

The measurement of the program's worth should address important questions. Following the program evaluation guidelines suggested by Rossi et al. (2018), key considerations include the nature and scope of the problems addressed by the program, justification for new or modified social programs, identification of feasible interventions to significantly reduce the problem, determination of the appropriate target population, assessment of intervention reach, evaluation of implementation quality, and examination of cost-effectiveness and benefit analysis. In the twenty-first century, evaluation research has become an integral part of routine activities at all levels of government organizations, non-government organizations, and public schemes (United Nations, 2017). It plays a significant role in shaping social policies, contributing to revisions and reforms in social programs. Evaluation is particularly crucial when resources are constrained, and evidence is required for decision-making regarding program concentration and prioritization (Sorensen & Grove, 1977).

Even though measuring the relationship between public resources and public values by the government is a complex process, it can be accomplished by comparing the expenses allocated to public resources with the anticipated or actual public value generated by a specific project. It is important to note that the impacts of the project on different social groups may vary. To enhance the accuracy of measurement, assessors utilized tools such as cost-effectiveness analysis, which includes the following:

- Payback period (PB)
- Net present value (NPV)
- Internal rate of return (IRR)
- Benefit-cost (B/C) ratio.

Evaluation of the Projects' Impact

The evaluation of a project's impact is commonly referred to as impact evaluation (IE). IE aims to determine the extent to which the impact can be attributed or causally linked to a specific project, program, policy, or other factors. It can be employed to evaluate projects of various scales, ranging from large-scale initiatives to targeted projects such as classroom learning outcomes. IE focuses on assessing the gains achieved through initiatives compared to the pre-existing conditions. It not only examines whether the project's objectives were achieved but also helps understand the mechanisms through which the impacts were generated (Thomas & Chindarkar, 2019).

Measuring a project's impact involves examining the process of transforming inputs into outcomes that deliver public value. Four key components are used to analyze a project's impact: localism, performance, logistics, and legitimacy.

When conducting impact evaluation, consideration must be given to selecting the most suitable method for evaluating a particular program. Thomas and Chindarkar (2019) propose important questions to guide this process, including: What resources are available, and what constraints exist? Who are the eligible units, and how are they selected? What is the nature and stage of the program being evaluated? Which outcomes are of interest? The outcomes or indicators can be measured using the SMART acronym, which stands for specific, measurable, attributable, realistic, and time-bound (Table 9.1).

The assessors then analyzed and evaluated the projects by developing an evaluation framework based on the collected data-complete research reports and research participants. Then, a systematic process and methodology for data analysis were employed as illustrated in framework (Table 9.2).

In addition, to analyze the quality, outputs, outcomes, and impacts of the research projects, the assessors set up indicators used as evaluation criteria, as illustrated in Table 9.3.

The analysis of the overall evaluation of the projects is as follows:

(1) Analysis of the sub-projects in every aspect including:
   - Human resource development
   - Education system
   - Improving economic status
   - Project worth
   - Project impact
   - Project sustainability.
(2) Classify the scoring criteria in every aspect into 5 levels (5 = Highest, 0 = No results found).
(3) Analysis of fieldwork data (e.g., the interview of the project director, researchers, research participants, relevant personnel, etc.), research report, other relevant documents.
(4) Present the overall analysis and analyze the results descriptively using diagrams and include the analysis and recommendations and suggestions from the assessors.

Table 9.1 Methodology to evaluate human resource development projects and policies

Assessment issues	Indicators	Sources of information	Tools	Data analysis	Results
1. Country's development of human resources is in accordance with the regional current situation of human resource development	**Content coverage and coherence of the projects**	• Complete research reports • Directors of the projects	• Data analysis record • Interview framework • Focus group discussion framework	• Content analysis	• Containing data indicating competencies and opportunities for human resource development as well as mechanisms to support good health, intellect, stability, and equality • Showing signs of changes in the practice of personnel relating to their wellbeing and environment
	Project worth • Financial value (budget, staff, management system) • Public value (prosperity, equality, good health)	• Complete research reports • Directors of the projects • Research project participants	• Data analysis record • Interview framework • Focus group discussion framework	• Statistical analysis • Content analysis	• Containing data indicating quality and factors applied in research • Containing data reflecting the public worth

(continued)

Table 9.1 (continued)

Assessment issues	Indicators	Sources of information	Tools	Data analysis	Results
	Project impact • The project coordination was carried out appropriately and systematically • The project was linked to the context of each area • The project was achievable under the laws and regulations with concrete results supported by empirical evidence	• Complete research reports • Directors of the projects • Research project participants	• Interview framework for the project director • Focus group discussion framework	• Content analysis	• Containing data and evidence of the logistics, legitimacy, performance, and localism aspects of knowledge application
	Project sustainability • Showing a tendency towards sustainable development	• Complete research reports • Directors of the projects • Research project participants	• Data analysis record • Interview framework • Focus group discussion framework	• Content analysis under the policy coherence for sustainable development framework	• Containing data reflecting the application of the knowledge to form policies and put them into practice

(continued)

Table 9.1 (continued)

Assessment issues	Indicators	Sources of information	Tools	Data analysis	Results
2. The development of the education system is in accordance with the current situation of ASEAN's human resource development	**Content coverage and coherence of the projects**	• Complete research reports • Directors of the projects	• Data analysis record • Interview framework • Focus group discussion framework	• Content analysis	• Containing data indicating competencies and opportunities for human resource development as well as mechanisms to support good health, intellect, stability, and equality • Showing signs of changes in the practice of personnel relating to their wellbeing and environment
	Project worth • Financial value (budget, staff, management system) • Public value (prosperity, equality, good health)	• Complete research reports • Directors of the projects • Research project participants	• Data analysis record • Interview framework • Focus group discussion framework	• Statistical analysis • Content analysis	• Containing data indicating quality and factors applied in research • Containing data reflecting the public worth

(continued)

Table 9.1 (continued)

Assessment issues	Indicators	Sources of information	Tools	Data analysis	Results
	Project impact • The project coordination was carried out appropriately and systematically • The project was linked to the context of each area • The project was achievable under the laws and regulations with concrete results supported by empirical evidence	• Complete research reports • Directors of the projects • Research project participants	• Interview framework for the project director • Focus group discussion framework	• Content analysis	• Containing data and evidence of the logistics, legitimacy, performance, and localism aspects of knowledge application
	Project sustainability • Showing a tendency towards sustainable development	• Complete research reports • Directors of the projects • Research project participants	• Data analysis record • Interview framework • Focus group discussion framework	• Content analysis under the policy coherence for sustainable development framework	• Containing data reflecting the application of the knowledge to form policies and put them into practice

(continued)

Table 9.1 (continued)

Assessment issues	Indicators	Sources of information	Tools	Data analysis	Results
3. The development of opportunities for improving economic status of labourers is in accordance with the current situation of ASEAN's human resource development	**Content coverage and coherence of the projects**	• Complete research reports • Directors of the projects	• Data analysis record • Interview framework • Focus group discussion framework	• Content analysis	• Containing data indicating competencies and opportunities for human resource development as well as mechanisms to support good health, intellect, stability, and equality • Showing signs of changes in the practice of personnel relating to their wellbeing and environment
	Project worth • Financial value (budget, staff, management system) • Public value (prosperity, equality, good health)	• Complete research reports • Directors of the projects • Research project participants	• Data analysis record • Interview framework • Focus group discussion framework	• Statistical analysis • Content analysis	• Containing data indicating quality and factors applied in research • Containing data reflecting the public worth

(continued)

Table 9.1 (continued)

Assessment issues	Indicators	Sources of information	Tools	Data analysis	Results
	Project impact • The project coordination was carried out appropriately and systematically • The project was linked to the context of each area • The project was achievable under the laws and regulations with concrete results supported by empirical evidence	• Complete research reports • Directors of the projects • Research project participants	• Interview framework for the project director • Focus group discussion framework	• Content analysis	• Containing data and evidence of the logistics, legitimacy, performance, and localism aspects of knowledge application
	Project sustainability • Showing a tendency towards sustainable development	• Complete research reports • Directors of the projects • Research project participants	• Data analysis record • Interview framework • Focus group discussion framework	• Content analysis under the policy coherence for sustainable development framework	• Containing data reflecting the application of the knowledge to form policies and put them into practice

(continued)

Table 9.1 (continued)

Assessment issues	Indicators	Sources of information	Tools	Data analysis	Results
4. Achievement of Thailand Research Fund in providing grants	**Content coverage and coherence of the projects**	• Complete research reports • Directors of the projects	• Data analysis record • Interview framework • Focus group discussion framework	• Content analysis	• Relevant to the results in issues 1–3
	Project worth • Financial value (budget, staff, management system) • Public value (prosperity, equality, good health)	• Complete research reports • Directors of the projects • Research project participants	• Data analysis record • Interview framework • Focus group discussion framework	• Statistical analysis • Content analysis	• Relevant to the results in issues 1–3

(continued)

Table 9.1 (continued)

Assessment issues	Indicators	Sources of information	Tools	Data analysis	Results
	Project impact • The project coordination was carried out appropriately and systematically • The project was linked to the context of each area • The project was achievable under the laws and regulations with concrete results supported by empirical evidence	• Complete research reports • Directors of the projects • Research project participants	• Interview framework for the project director • Focus group discussion framework	• Content analysis	• Relevant to the results in issues 1–3
	Project sustainability • Showing a tendency towards sustainable development	• Complete research reports • Directors of the projects • Research project participants	• Data analysis record • Interview framework • Focus group discussion framework	• Content analysis under the policy coherence for sustainable development framework	• Relevant to the results in issues 1–3

Table 9.2 A framework for data collection divided by data sources

Projects classified by research activities	Data sources and data acquisition methods					
	Research reports	Research project manager	Research participants	Research sites	Related working units	Stakeholders
Action research	S	I	I	K	I	F
Secondary data analysis	S	I				
Survey research	S	I	I	K	I	F
Case study (lesson learned)	S	I	I	K	I	F

Note *S* synthesis; *I* interview; *F* focus group; *K* focus group and observation

Table 9.3 List of indicators used as evaluation criteria

Key assessment criteria	Secondary criteria (1)	Secondary criteria (2)	Indicator
Content coverage and coherence of the projects	Human resource development	Physical aspect	80% coherence
		Mental aspect	80% coherence
		Social aspect	80% coherence
		Intellectual aspect	80% coherence
	Education system development	Ideology change	80% coherence
		Change in schooling	80% coherence
		Change in expectations	80% coherence
	Increase opportunities for improving economic status of laborers in ASEAN context	Opportunities for improving economic status	80% coherence
		Strengths and abilities to compete in the global market	80% coherence
Project worth	Public worth		80% coherence
	Financial value		80% coherence
Project impact	Logistics		80% coherence
	Localism		80% coherence
	Legitimacy		80% coherence
	Performance		80% coherence
Project sustainability	PCSD framework		80% coherence
		Coherence with the research program	100% coherence

Conclusion

In conclusion, Chap. 6 of "Methodological Framework for Evaluating Human Resource Research" offers a comprehensive understanding of the evaluation process and its sequential steps. By focusing on goal setting, objective establishment, method selection, and data analysis, the chapter provides valuable insights into how to conduct a rigorous and reliable evaluation. The key elements and components of the framework outlined in the chapter contribute to the systematic and structured approach to evaluation, enabling evaluators to obtain accurate and meaningful findings. The emphasis on systematic and rigorous data collection underscores the significance of obtaining reliable and valid data, which forms the foundation for credible evaluation outcomes. By following the methodology and principles outlined in this chapter, evaluators can enhance the quality and credibility of their human resource research evaluations, ultimately leading to informed decision-making and improved organizational practices.

References

Aliverdi, R., Naeni, L. M., & Salehipour, A. (2013). Monitoring project duration and cost in a construction project by applying statistical quality control charts. *International Journal of Project Management, 31*(3), 411–423.

Angel, B. F., Duffey, M., & Belyea, M. (2000). An evidence-based project for evaluating strategies to improve knowledge acquisition and critical-thinking performance in nursing students. *Journal of Nursing Education, 39*(5), 219–228.

Bottrill, M. C., & Pressey, R. L. (2012). The effectiveness and evaluation of conservation planning. *Conservation Letters, 5*(6), 407–420.

Creswell, J. W., Fetters, M. D., & Ivankova, N. V. (2004). Designing a mixed methods study in primary care. *The Annals of Family Medicine, 2*(1), 7–12.

Di Baldassarre, G., Sivapalan, M., Rusca, M., Cudennec, C., Garcia, M., Kreibich, H., Konar, M., Mondino, E., Mård, J., Pande, S., Sanderson, M. R., Tian, F., Viglione, A., Wei, J., Wei, Y., Yu, D. J., Srinivasan, V., & Blöschl, G. (2019). Sociohydrology: Scientific challenges in addressing the sustainable development goals. *Water Resources Research, 55*(8), 6327–6355.

Johnson, J. M., & Rowlands, T. (2012). The interpersonal dynamics of in-depth interviewing. In *The SAGE handbook of interview research: The complexity of the craft* (pp. 99–113).

Khalife, S., & Hamzeh, F. (2019). An integrative approach to analyze the attributes shaping the dynamic nature of value in AEC. *Lean Construction Journal*, 91–104.

Lakner, C., & Milanovic, B. (2013). *Global income distribution: from the fall of the Berlin Wall to the great recession* (Policy Research Working Paper No. 6719). World Bank, Washington, DC.

Rossi, P. H., Lipsey, M. W., & Henry, G. T. (2018). *Evaluation: A systematic approach.* Sage.

Sorensen, J. E., & Grove, H. D. (1977). Cost-outcome and cost-effectiveness analysis. Emerging nonprofit performance evaluation techniques. *The Accounting Review, 52*(3), 658–675.

Stufflebeam, D. L. (2000). The CIPP model for evaluation. In *Evaluation models: Viewpoints on educational and human services evaluation* (pp. 279–317).

Thomas, V., & Chindarkar, N. (2019). *Economic evaluation of sustainable development.* Springer Nature.

United Nations. (2017). *Evaluation handbook guidance for designing, conducting and using independent evaluation at UNODC.* United Nations Office on Drugs and Crime.

Vandenberg, R. J., & Lance, C. E. (2000). A review and synthesis of the measurement invariance literature: Suggestions, practices, and recommendations for organizational research. *Organizational Research Methods, 3*(1), 4–70.

Veltri, N. F., Webb, H. W., Matveev, A. G., & Zapatero, E. G. (2011). Curriculum mapping as a tool for continuous improvement of IS curriculum. *Journal of Information Systems Education, 22*(1), 31.

Wirtz, B. W., & Müller, W. M. (2021). A meta-analysis of smart city research and its future research implications. *International Public Management Review, 21*(2), 18–39.

Chapter 10
Practical Illustration and Future Direction of the Integrated Evaluation Model

Introduction

In this book, we present a model for evaluating projects based on seven aspects: the three key components are a long and healthy life, education and knowledge, and a decent standard of living, and the Influencing contextual factors namely, content coverage and coherence of the projects, measurement of project worth, evaluation of project impact, evaluation of project sustainability.

Our evaluation model focuses on determining the outcomes and impacts of human development research projects, as we deem that human resource development (HRD) is closely tied to human well-being, and that development strategies should be multi-dimensional and integrated, rather than solely focused on economic benefits and income generation. Additionally, we present a methodology for project evaluation based on an integrated evaluation model approach (Chokevivat, 2009).

This chapter provides an overview of the investigation and evaluation of the research program, highlighting the diverse aspects of HRD in both labor welfare and educational development (a long and healthy life and education and knowledge aspects). The data collection involved structured interviews conducted with project directors of the research program and projects, focus group discussions involving research teams and participants, and field notes. Data collection was carried out using various social research methods, including document analysis, focus groups, and in-depth interviews.

Background of the Research Program

The research program being evaluated is a critical component of Thailand's national human resource strategies and is aligned with economic policies. Additionally, the program serves as a foundation for manpower development and has been an integral

N. Kiettikunwong and P. Narot, *Determining Outcomes and Impacts of Human Resource Development Programs*, https://doi.org/10.1007/978-981-97-0395-1_10

part of Thailand's strategic development plans, focusing on innovation and digitalization. The program comprises two sets of research projects. The first set focuses on labor welfare and human resource development, specifically addressing the aspect of promoting a long and healthy life. These projects include: (1) Examining the relationship between human capital and labor productivity in the manufacturing sector, (2) Investigating the impact of skeletal and muscular system-related diseases among workers in the warehouse and retail industry to enhance occupational health and safety in the workplace, and (3) Addressing occupational health and safety concerns for migrant labor in the fishing industry.

The second set of the program focused on educational and knowledge development for human advancement, specifically addressing the education and knowledge aspect. It encompassed the following cases: (1) A case study of successful education management models in small schools, (2) Lessons learned from experiences in small-sized schools, (3) Management of multi-sector cooperation in education for local communities, (4) Development of national education testing and quality assessment at the basic education level, (5) Quality assurance in sociology and anthropology, (6) Decentralization of education to local administration organizations, (7) Situations and guidelines for enhancing labor's vocational rehabilitation and retraining, and (8) Improvement of semi-skilled and middle-skilled workers in business organizations following the sufficiency economy philosophy, particularly those without a vocational institution background.

Translating Outcomes and Impacts

Based on the integrated evaluation model revealed the outcomes and impacts of the HRD programs. In the evaluation of the research program on labor welfare and human resource development, the first case focused on analyzing the causes of the low levels of innovation investment in the industrial business sector in Thailand. The analysis found that the major contributing factors were the high cost of innovation (43.6%) and a shortage of knowledgeable personnel (42.7%), indicating a quantitative and qualitative scarcity of human resources in the country (Kilenthong, 2014). To address this, skilled labor development and labor productivity improvement were identified as crucial aspects of the national strategy.

The project examined human capital and labor productivity in Thailand's industrial sector at two levels. Firstly, individual human capital development was analyzed, considering factors such as education and training, and the outcomes were evaluated in terms of wages and employment. Secondly, macroeconomic data was analyzed to study the connection between human capital and the labor market. The project utilized various data sources, including firm surveys, productivity and investment climate surveys, and the labor force survey conducted by the National Statistics Office between 2007 and 2011 (National Statistical Office, 2015). The findings indicated that the majority of workers in the industrial sector (67.6%) had a high school diploma and a vocational school certificate, while 20.4% held a degree, and 12% had a primary school diploma. Additionally, a significant proportion of firms (65–75%) employed labor from vocational institutes, highlighting the project's alignment with policy objectives.

Regarding project worth, one noteworthy finding was that the labor force possessed strong skills to address labor shortages in the manufacturing sector. However, there was a mismatch between the quality of higher education graduates and the needs of employers, emphasizing the importance of addressing this issue in both education and human resource development. The project also provided valuable information on opportunities for improving economic status and human resource development. For instance, technical staff, such as scientists, analysts, and IT technicians, constituted only 4% of the total permanent labor force. The study also revealed that in-house training (63.5%) and outsourced training (64.1%) were prevalent, with larger firms placing greater emphasis on staff training compared to smaller ones.

The analysis demonstrated that the employment of higher education graduates contributed to increased labor productivity, outweighing the cost of rising wages. However, the impact was found to be short-term. It was concluded that labor training was a beneficial activity, offering advantages rather than increasing costs. The research report highlighted the mismatch between the skills possessed by workers at different educational levels and the needs of the labor market. There was a particular deficiency in English skills, followed by technology skills, arithmetic skills, and innovative and creative skills necessary for cognitive development and enhancement of life skills such as leadership, problem-solving, and socialization (Pholphirul & Rukumnuaykit, 2013). These findings provide a basis for improving economic status and well-being of the labor force. The information generated from this project can be utilized for human resource development and serve as a valuable resource for policymakers and future evaluators, not only within Thailand but also for other ASEAN countries.

The study focused on occupational health and safety for migrant labor in the fishing industry. The project aimed to examine the occupational health and safety conditions of laborers in the fishing industry and develop a model for occupational safety and health risk assessment. This was achieved by conducting a walk-through survey and job safety analysis to assess the occupational and health risks faced by laborers working on Thai fishing boats. The project's content coverage and coherence were supported by the literature review, which highlighted that the labor workforce primarily consisted of Burmese workers who lacked adequate environmental well-being.

The project's worth and impacts remained evident even after a five-year follow-up. Key informants, including the head of the provincial labor office, fishing boat owners, port directors, and workmen leaders, participated in focus group interviews. They expressed a positive attitude towards improving occupational health and safety, considering it as an investment to enhance the work environment, foster better employer-worker relationships, and increase labor productivity. The sustainability of the project was reinforced by the fishing boat owners' commitment to the safety of their workers, with safety being a fundamental aspect of their management approach. However, it is important to note that while these positive activities were aligned with the project's content and coverage, it cannot be concluded that all the positive impacts were solely due to the project intervention.

The next case in this program focused on the promotion of occupational health and safety in the workplace, specifically investigating the impacts of skeletal and muscular system-related diseases among workers in the warehouse and retail industry. The project aimed to enhance skills and create a fair and enriching society, ensuring stability in workers' lives and providing comprehensive and equal social protection. The project's goal was to increase labor productivity by fostering happiness in the workplace and studying occupational health and safety among workers in the warehouse and retail sector (Gavin & Mason, 2004).

The content coverage of this project was derived from document analysis, which revealed that workplace illnesses were caused by factors such as prolonged repetitive work, time constraints without adequate tools and equipment, lack of safety measures, and employers solely focusing on increasing productivity by offering monetary incentives to workers who outperform others.

The evaluation was carried out an assessment by conducting a comprehensive field study, employing diverse sources and methodologies. Key informants and stakeholders, including the project coordinator (an NGO), factory owners, the head of the labor group, and the workmen, were involved in interviews and focus group discussions. These stakeholders were directly impacted by the intervention. The information gathered from the focus group discussions revealed the project's worth. Prior to the project's implementation, workers faced difficulties in accessing healthcare rights when they fell ill due to concerns about their work record under Thailand's Zero Accident Campaign. Some workmen had limited access to legal rights, workmen's compensation benefits, and treatment from occupational physicians. The project's impacts were confirmed by the introduction of occupational health and safety suggestions to workplaces, government agencies, and educational institutions. Importantly, employers became aware that promoting a happy workplace environment could enhance labor productivity. The results also demonstrated that involving various stakeholder groups not only aligned with the National Development Plan in HRD but also showcased the impact and sustainability of the project. The knowledge gained from the intervention was shared with relevant organizations, leading to the implementation of health and safety legal measures and benefits for the workmen. This intervention resulted in improved health and well-being for the labor force.

Another project in this program focused on increasing labor efficiency and productivity. The evaluation team investigated the case that synthesized knowledge related to skill improvement for workers who did not graduate from vocational institutions in business organizations following the sufficiency economy philosophy. Various strategies were implemented, including establishing a mentoring system, providing training both within and outside the workplace, supporting workers in pursuing higher education, promoting teamwork, encouraging self-improvement, problem-solving skills, and enhancing knowledge and the ability to care for families amid economic uncertainty. This approach aligned with the national policy, which aimed to improve human resource development and, consequently, enhance economic status.

Comparing the labor productivity index of business organizations following the sufficiency economy philosophy with the industry structure from 2009 to 2013, it was found that the labor productivity index initially lagged behind but consistently and significantly surpassed the industry structure in 2013 (National Statistical Office, 2015). In addition to education and training, creating favorable working conditions and an atmosphere that enables work-life balance played a crucial role in developing and enhancing the quality of these workers. The project's impacts and sustainability can be observed through the textbook produced using the project's knowledge, which is used in vocational colleges, as well as the handbook distributed to industry administrators and workmen.

The second set of programs focuses on educational and knowledge-based human development cases related to human resource development. The first case examines learners' efficiency and standards in the school system. A documentary analysis compared predictor variables that might have influenced the TIMSS 2011 scores of ASEAN and East Asian students. This case emphasizes education knowledge to promote skill development. The content coverage aligns with human resource development goals and is consistent with the other sub-projects. The knowledge base of schoolteachers and administrators should help students recognize their own potential and abilities and develop a positive attitude towards learning. Science teachers, in particular, play a crucial role in guiding students, using instructional scaffolding, and fostering independent knowledge-seeking to ensure academic success. In the initial stages of learning, teachers should provide clear guidelines, demonstrate processes, and offer immediate feedback to students. Understanding students' backgrounds also aids in planning and organizing learning at home and creating a friendly and supportive learning environment. The distribution of resources and funding in small schools should be equitable and accessible to all students (Kajornsin, 2016). Sustainable development, intensive professional development, an effective follow-up system, and efforts to reduce educational inequality are key factors that can lead to higher academic performance and student quality. These findings contribute to the promotion of a better life, education, and knowledge. Regarding the project's worth, impacts, and sustainability, it can be concluded that 90% of the projects were deemed worthwhile, created impacts, and exhibited a tendency towards sustainable development.

The case study presents a successful model of education management in small schools based on multi-sector cooperation in education for local communities. It demonstrates alignment with the goals and objectives of lifelong learning and a healthy life, making a significant impact on education and human development. The sustainability aspect is evident through its coherence with sustainability policies.

The case of national education testing and quality assessment at the basic education level strongly supports content coverage. The case related to quality assurance in sociology and anthropology focuses on education and contributes to knowledge and knowledge. The case of developing accreditation for occupational skill standards in vocational education qualifications demonstrates content coverage aligned with the project's goals and objectives, promoting a healthy life, education, and knowledge. This case showcases impacts and sustainability through the development of coursework, textbooks, and curriculum for students (Pitiyanuwat et al., 2013).

The case that focuses on improving semi-skilled and middle-skilled workers who did not graduate from a vocational institution in business organizations following the sufficiency economy philosophy fulfills the aspects of the integrated evaluation model in terms of content coverage, coherence, and consistency with other projects. It contributes to a healthy life, education, and knowledge, and exhibits sustainability.

Lastly, the case aimed at educational development through the decentralization of education under the management of local administration organizations emphasizes social reconstructionism. The project's content and coverage align with goals related to a healthy life and demonstrate coherence and consistency among subprojects. This case highlights the importance of promoting informal education for all ages and genders, creating learning spaces for independent, group, and collaborative learning in communities, and providing opportunities for local people to establish their own learning resources. These aspects contribute to education, knowledge, and lifelong learning. In terms of sustainability, this case fosters informal learning by offering opportunities for learning from various resources and empowering students to become lifelong learners. The impact of the case is evident in schools becoming an integral part of the community, addressing community problems, and nurturing community engagement. This leads to a healthy life and sustainability of the case.

The establishment of multilateral partnerships in this case proves beneficial in fostering public participation in developing plans for informal education, setting learning standards for the community, developing a school system and mechanism to support local curriculum learning management, and encouraging students to engage in public service activities. The evidence from the case confirms the coherence of policies for sustainable development.

Important Notion

Notably, one of the major challenges in assessing the impact of a case is determining whether the project's success is solely attributable to its own efforts or influenced by external factors or interventions from other programs. When conducting impact assessments, evaluators need to thoroughly investigate the program's recipients and determine if they have received the intended intervention (Rossi et al., 2018). In this evaluation process, the evaluators employed an integrated model approach to assess the outcomes and impacts of the programs, gathering data from stakeholders who were recipients of the cases.

A significant lesson learned from the evaluation process is the need to adapt and tailor evaluations to align with the project and situational contexts. For instance, in the evaluation of the fishing boat workmen's health risks and safety project, the evaluation team had to make adjustments considering the appropriate timeframe and the dynamics of the economics, as the period between the project implementation and evaluation was quite long. The evaluation program aimed to provide program information for the funding agency, and through modification, the evaluation team obtained supporting information for the development of fishing boat workmen's health risks and safety from new groups of key informants who were not direct recipients of the research project. However, these informants were situated in the area where the case was implemented and possessed direct experiences related to the study's content coverage.

The information obtained from these various stakeholders provided valuable insight and clear evidence that the development in this area resulted from the collaborative efforts of multiple stakeholders, including the Department of Marine, Provincial Fisheries Department, local administrative subdistricts, and NGOs involved in immigrants' registration and welfare. Therefore, it is crucial to utilize multiple sources such as research reports, monographs, website publications, key informant interviews, and group discussions to gather evidence and verbal information and conduct systematic analysis. These approaches are useful and more relevant to the situation, and when data is triangulated, the case findings gain stronger support through multiple sources of evidence. The integrated model analysis, including literature review, document analysis, open-ended interviews, focus-group interviews, and structured interviews, is essential in supporting the findings and employing data triangulation, which enhances the construct validity of the study (Yin, 2014).

Final Thoughts

Authors strive their best to highlight the significance of the integrated evaluation model presented in the book. The book underscores the effectiveness of the integrated evaluation model in assessing the success and effectiveness of human resource research interventions while also acknowledging any limitations or challenges that may arise in its application. It provides recommendations for further research and improvement in the field. Model effectiveness refers to the overall performance and capability of a model to achieve its intended objectives and deliver meaningful outcomes. It encompasses various aspects that determine the model's ability to efficiently and accurately solve specific problems or tasks. Some key elements contributing to model effectiveness are highlighted. The developed integrated model demonstrates its effectiveness in producing correct and crucial results. While it may not have the ability to generalize in certain aspects, its interpretability can be enhanced. Interpretability refers to the ability to explain or understand the reasoning behind the model's predictions or decisions, enabling stakeholders to trust and comprehend its outputs. Additionally, the real-world impact of the model is measured by its impact in real-world applications. An effective model produces outcomes that align with desired objectives, contributes to decision-making processes, improves efficiency, and has a societal impact.

Limitations and Challenges of the Model

When assessing the model, the issues of limitations and challenges of a model is a key aspect. It's important to recognize potential areas where the model may fall short or face difficulties. Understanding these limitations helps set realistic expectations and guides efforts for improvement. Here are some common limitations and challenges that models may encounter: (1) Data quality and availability: Models heavily rely on the quality and availability of data for training and validation. Insufficient or low-quality data can lead to biased or inaccurate results, limiting the model's effectiveness. Data scarcity or data imbalance can also pose challenges in this evaluation model. (2) Model may struggle with overfitting, where they perform exceedingly well on the obtained data but fail to generalize to unseen data. Conversely, underfitting occurs when a model fails to capture the underlying patterns in the data, resulting in over-claiming the success of the program. Balancing model complexity and regularization techniques can help mitigate these issues. (3) In general, the model's effectiveness heavily relies on the choice and relevance of input features. Inadequate feature engineering or selection may lead to poor performance or the inclusion of irrelevant or redundant features. Identifying meaningful features and extracting useful information is crucial for model effectiveness. (4) Models often make assumptions about the underlying data distribution or relationships, and these assumptions may not always hold true in real-world scenarios. Violation of these assumptions can lead to diminished performance and inaccurate predictions (Dhar & Varshney, 2011; Elices et al., 2002). It is crucial to be aware of these limitations and challenges when working with models. Ongoing evaluation, continuous improvement, and addressing these limitations contribute to the development of more effective and reliable models.

Challenges in Human Development Evaluation Model

Evaluating human development is a complex and multidimensional task that presents several challenges. Human development evaluation aims to assess the well-being and progress of individuals and societies in various aspects of life. Here are some challenges associated with evaluating human development: (1) Multidimensionality Human development encompasses multiple dimensions, including education, health, income, social inclusion, gender equality, and environmental sustainability. Capturing and measuring these diverse dimensions comprehensively and accurately poses a significant challenge. (2) Data Availability and Quality: Obtaining reliable and up-to-date data for human development evaluation can be challenging, especially in less-developed regions or marginalized populations. Inadequate data infrastructure, data gaps, and lack of standardization can hinder the assessment of human development indicators. (3) Subjectivity and Perceptions: Evaluating human development often involves subjective aspects, such as assessing quality of life, happiness, or satisfaction. Different individuals or communities may have varying perceptions of what constitutes development or well-being, making it challenging to have universally applicable evaluation metrics. (4) Contextual Factors: Human development is influenced by a wide range of contextual factors, including cultural, social, economic, and political conditions. These contextual factors introduce complexities and variations that need to be accounted for during evaluation. (5) Equity and Inequality: Assessing human development involves addressing issues of equity and inequality. Evaluating whether development outcomes are equitably distributed among different social groups, regions, or genders requires considering disparities in access, opportunities, and outcomes. (6) Long-term Impacts: Human development evaluation should consider the long-term impacts of policies, interventions, and societal changes. Identifying the sustained effects and unintended consequences of development initiatives can be challenging due to complex causal relationships and time lags. (7) Cultural Sensitivity and Diversity: Evaluating human development across diverse cultures, contexts, and value systems requires cultural sensitivity. Understanding and respecting diverse perspectives and local contexts is crucial to ensure valid and meaningful evaluation outcomes. (8) Interdisciplinary Approach: Evaluating human development requires an interdisciplinary approach that incorporates insights from various fields such as economics, sociology, psychology, and environmental science. Integrating diverse disciplines and methodologies while maintaining coherence and comparability can be demanding (Davis, 2017; Heckman & Mosso, 2014).

Addressing these challenges requires a nuanced and adaptive evaluation framework that acknowledges the complexity and context-specific nature of human development. Incorporating participatory approaches, engaging local stakeholders, and continuously refining evaluation methodologies can contribute to more accurate and comprehensive assessments of human development (Conger & Donnellan, 2007).

Improvement for Human Development Evaluation

Improving human development evaluation requires a multidisciplinary approach, collaboration among various stakeholders, and a commitment to continuous learning and improvement. By addressing these areas of improvement, the evaluation process can provide more robust, reliable, and actionable information to guide policy formulation and decision-making towards sustainable human development (Laycock et al., 2017). Improvement for human development evaluation refers to efforts aimed at enhancing the effectiveness, efficiency, and relevance of the evaluation process and methodologies used to assess human development. The goal is to refine and strengthen the evaluation frameworks, tools, and approaches to generate more accurate, comprehensive, and actionable insights into the progress and well-being of individuals and societies. Some key areas of improvement for human development evaluation can be as follows: (1) Enhanced Data Collection and Analysis: Improve data collection methods, data quality, and data integration across multiple sources.

Invest in new technologies, data science techniques, and partnerships to ensure reliable and up-to-date data for evaluation purposes. (2) Comprehensive Indicator Selection: Continuously review and update the set of indicators used for evaluation to capture the multidimensional nature of human development. Ensure that indicators represent various aspects such as education, health, income, social inclusion, gender equality, and environmental sustainability. (3) Contextual Relevance: Develop evaluation frameworks and methodologies that are contextually relevant, considering cultural, social, economic, and political factors. Incorporate local perspectives and specificities to ensure that evaluation models align with the needs and priorities of the communities being assessed. (4) Holistic Approach: Adopt holistic evaluation frameworks that account for the interconnections between different dimensions of human development. Consider composite indices or dashboards that provide a comprehensive overview of progress across multiple indicators. (5) Participatory Engagement: Engage stakeholders, including local communities, policymakers, civil society organizations, and experts, in the evaluation process. Foster participatory approaches that involve stakeholders at various stages, ensuring their inputs are valued and incorporated into the evaluation framework. (6) Longitudinal Studies: Conduct longitudinal studies to track changes in human development over time. This allows for the identification of trends, assessment of the impact of policies and interventions, and understanding of long-term outcomes. (7) Improved Analytical Techniques: Utilize advanced analytical techniques, such as multilevel analysis, econometric modeling, and data visualization, to extract meaningful insights from evaluation data. These techniques help uncover complex relationships, disparities, and patterns within the data. (8) Addressing Equity and Inclusion: Develop evaluation models that explicitly consider equity and inclusion aspects. Assess the distributional impacts of development policies and interventions across different social groups, regions, or socioeconomic backgrounds. (9) Transparency and Accountability: Foster transparency in the evaluation process by clearly documenting methodologies, data sources, and assumptions. Ensure accountability by making evaluation findings accessible to policymakers, researchers, and the public, facilitating informed decision-making. (10) Continuous Learning and Adaptation: Treat human development evaluation as an iterative and learning-oriented process. Continuously learn from past evaluations, incorporate feedback, and adapt the evaluation model to incorporate new insights, emerging challenges, and best practices (Madon, 2004; Nussbaum, 2006).

Future Direction for Integrated Evaluation Model

Future studies can contribute to advancing HRD evaluation practices, refining models and frameworks, and promoting evidence-based decision-making. The findings can inform the design, implementation, and evaluation of HRD interventions, ultimately leading to improved learning outcomes, employee performance, and organizational effectiveness (Steffensen et al., 2019). These research can be in the flowing aspects: (1) Emerging Technologies and Learning Methods: Explore the integration of emerging technologies, such as virtual reality, artificial intelligence, and augmented reality, in HRD evaluation. Investigate how these technologies can enhance learning experiences, improve knowledge retention, and provide real-time feedback for performance improvement. (2) Personalized and Adaptive Learning: Investigate the effectiveness of personalized and adaptive learning approaches in HRD. Explore how customized learning pathways, tailored content, and adaptive assessments can enhance individual learning outcomes and performance. (3) Lifelong Learning and Continuous Development: Examine the impact of HRD interventions on lifelong learning and continuous development. Investigate strategies to promote a learning culture within organizations, support employees' self-directed learning, and assess the long-term impact of ongoing development initiatives. (4) Data Analytics and Learning Analytics: Utilize data analytics and learning analytics techniques to evaluate the effectiveness of HRD interventions. Explore how data-driven insights can inform instructional design, identify learning gaps, and optimize learning outcomes. (5) Assessment of Competencies and Skills: Develop robust methodologies for assessing competencies and skills acquired through HRD programs. Explore innovative approaches, such as competency-based assessments, performance simulations, and real-world projects, to evaluate the practical application of learned skills. (6) Impact on Employee Engagement and Well-being: Investigate the impact of HRD interventions on employee engagement, job satisfaction, and well-being. Examine how HRD programs can enhance motivation, foster a positive work environment, and contribute to employee resilience and mental health. (7) Leadership Development and Succession Planning: Examine the effectiveness of HRD interventions in developing leadership capabilities and supporting succession planning. Investigate the long-term impact of leadership development programs on organizational leadership capacity and performance. (8) Evaluation of Diversity and Inclusion Initiatives: Assess the effectiveness of HRD interventions in promoting diversity, equity, and inclusion within organizations. Explore the impact of diversity training, bias awareness programs, and inclusive leadership development on organizational culture and employee experiences. (9) Cross-Cultural and Global HRD Evaluation: Examine the effectiveness of HRD interventions in diverse cultural and global contexts. Investigate the transferability of HRD models across different cultural settings, assess the impact of cultural intelligence training, and explore the challenges and opportunities in global leadership development. (10) Evaluation of HRD Policies and Practices: Evaluate the effectiveness of HRD policies and practices at the organizational and national levels. Examine the impact of government initiatives, regulatory frameworks, and funding mechanisms on HRD outcomes and societal development. (11) Ethics and Social Responsibility in HRD Evaluation: Explore the ethical considerations and social responsibility aspects of HRD evaluation. Investigate the ethical implications of data collection and analysis, ensure privacy and confidentiality, and assess the social impact and sustainability of HRD initiatives (Joo et al., 2013; Russ-Eft, 2014; Torraco, 2004).

However, model effectiveness can be enhanced through continual refinement and improvement. Models can undergo iterations of evaluation, feedback, and updates to address limitations, incorporate new data, and adapt to changing conditions.

By considering these elements of model effectiveness, stakeholders can assess the model's performance and make informed decisions regarding its deployment and improvement. This ensures that the model can be generalized and has the potential to be used in solving real-world problems.

References

Chokevivat, V. (2009). A study on the four dimensions of health. *Journal of Health Systems Research, 3*(3), 323–335.

Conger, R. D., & Donnellan, M. B. (2007). An interactionist perspective on the socioeconomic context of human development. *Annual Review of Psychology, 58*, 175–199.

Davis, T. J. (2017). Good governance as a foundation for sustainable human development in sub-Saharan Africa. *Third World Quarterly, 38*(3), 636–654.

Dhar, S., & Varshney, U. (2011). Challenges and business models for mobile location-based services and advertising. *Communications of the ACM, 54*(5), 121–128.

Elices, M. G. G. V., Guinea, G. V., Gomez, J., & Planas, J. (2002). The cohesive zone model: Advantages, limitations and challenges. *Engineering Fracture Mechanics, 69*(2), 137–163.

Gavin, J. H., & Mason, R. O. (2004). The virtuous organization: The value of happiness in the workplace. *Organizational Dynamics, 33*(4), 379–392.

Heckman, J. J., & Mosso, S. (2014). The economics of human development and social mobility. *Annual Review of Economics, 6*(1), 689–733.

Joo, B. K., McLean, G. N., & Yang, B. (2013). Creativity and human resource development: An integrative literature review and a conceptual framework for future research. *Human Resource Development Review, 12*(4), 390–421.

Kajornsin, B. (2016). *The Evaluation of outputs, outcomes, and impacts of local learning enrichment network program of children*. The Thailand Research Fund.

Kilenthong, W. (2014). Finance and inequality in Thailand. In *Bank of Thailand (BOT) Symposium 2014*, September 17, 2014, Bank of Thailand's Headquarters, Bangkok.

Laycock, A., Bailie, J., Matthews, V., Cunningham, F., Harvey, G., Percival, N., & Bailie, R. (2017). A developmental evaluation to enhance stakeholder engagement in a wide-scale interactive project disseminating quality improvement data: Study protocol for a mixed-methods study. *British Medical Journal Open, 7*(7), e016341.

Madon, S. (2004). Evaluating the developmental impact of e-governance initiatives: An exploratory framework. *The Electronic Journal of Information Systems in Developing Countries, 20*(1), 1–13.

National Statistical Office. (2015). *Household socio-economic survey throughout the Kingdom B.E. 2558*. Statistical Forecasting Bureau.

Nussbaum, M. C. (2006). Education and democratic citizenship: Capabilities and quality education. *Journal of Human Development, 7*(3), 385–395.

Pholphirul, P., & Rukumnuaykit, P. (2013). *Human capital and labor productivity in Thai manufacturers*. School of Development Economics and International College, National Institute of Development Administration (NIDA).

Pitiyanuwat, S., Pipatsuntikul, P., Wudthayagorn, J., & Pitiyanuwat, T. (2013). *Development of national education testing and educational quality assurance at the basic education level*. Institute for Research and Quality Development Foundation.

Rossi, P. H., Lipsey, M. W., & Henry, G. T. (2018). *Evaluation: A systematic approach*. Sage.

Russ-Eft, D. F. (2014). Human resource development, evaluation, and sustainability: What are the relationships? *Human Resource Development International, 17*(5), 545–559.

Steffensen, D. S., Jr., Ellen, B. P., III., Wang, G., & Ferris, G. R. (2019). Putting the "management" back in human resource management: A review and agenda for future research. *Journal of Management, 45*(6), 2387–2418.

Torraco, R. J. (2004). Challenges and choices for theoretical research in human resource development. *Human Resource Development Quarterly, 15*(2), 171–188.

Yin, R. K. (2014). *Case study research*. Sage.

The manufacturer's authorised representative in the EU is Springer Nature Customer Service Centre GmbH, Europaplatz 3, 69115 Heidelberg, Germany. If you have any concerns regarding our products, please contact ProductSafety@springernature.com

Printed and bound by CPI Group (UK) Ltd, Croydon, CR0 4YY

30/09/2026

02225309-0017